9780911982114
AF574888

Flov

vers: abstract form II

M. Benz

Published by
SAN JACINTO PUBLISHING CO.
P.O. Box 66254
Houston, Texas 77006

SAN JACINTO PUBLISHING CO.
P. O. Box 66254 Houston, Texas 77006

Library of Congress Catalog No. 78-65678
International Standard Book Number 0-911982-011-06

First Printing—1976 First Edition—FLOWERS: ABSTRACT FORM
Second Printing—1979 Second Edition—Revised FLOWERS: ABSTRACT FORM II

Manufactured in United States. Printed Brandt & Lawson. Layout Jim Hogg.

Chinese Bamboo Fence
See Text Page 146

Dedicated to:

*Those lovers of beauty who seek
Truth and Poetry in form and color.*

PLATE 1

PREFACE

The purpose of this book is to share with you the creativity of floral design — inspiration that springs from infinite being — that moment the subconscious mind spontaneously produces an idea.

It is imagination.
It is art.
It is involvement requiring action.

The culmination of ideas satisfies the yearning for completeness. It is art because it has reached the zenith — that stage of perfection as seen through the individual's eye. Art is beauty only in the Truths and feelings it conveys. When it is shared with another — when there is communication — an understanding between the artist and viewer — then a great sense of joy and fulfillment is experienced.

This book opens new horizons — new worlds — unlimited in time and space.

"Flowers
leave some of their fragrance
in the hand that bestows them".

Chinese Proverb

NATURE has perfection
in order to show that she is the image of God;
And defects to show that she is only His image.

Blaise Pascal

PAGAN RITES — *Hands rise in unison forming a bond of friendship before the pagan altar.*

ACKNOWLEDGMENTS:

A MUSE (1917)	Constantin Brancusi	–Museum of Fine Arts, Houston, Texas
UNTITLED (1964)	Tadasky	–Museum of Fine Arts, Houston, Texas
DRAWING A LESSON	Editorial Page	–Baltimore Sun
NIJINSKY (1913)	Auguste Rodin	–Collection of the author
REBOSA	Bonnie Seaman	–Collection of the author
SEA GULL	Bonnie Seaman	–Collection of the author
YANG-YIN	Bonnie Seaman	–Collection of the sculptor
CRUCIFIX (iron)	William S. McKenzie	–Collection of the author
REGATTA	William Coghlan	–Collection of the author
SEA GULLS	William Coghlan	–Collection of the author
NUDE	Virginia Pollack	–Collection of the author (Replica)
FIGURE–2	Haku Maki	–Collection of the author
THE WAY OF THE EAGLE	Clark Bronson	–Collection of the author
THE FALL OF MAN	Tom Baringer	–Collection of the author
Photography	M. Benz	
Editing	Bessie H. Eidson	

Drawing a Lesson

As Mrs. Klein told her first-graders to draw a picture of something for which they were thankful, she thought how little these children, the mixed offerings of a deteriorating neighborhood, actually had to be thankful for. She knew that most of the class would draw pictures of turkeys or of bountifully laden Thanksgiving tables. That was what they believed was expected of them.

What took Mrs. Klein aback was Douglas' picture. Douglas she looked upon as her true child of misery, so scrubby and forlorn, and so likely to be found close in her shadow as they went outside for recess. Douglas' drawing was simply this:

A hand, obviously, but whose hand? The class was captivated by the abstract image. "I think it must be the hand of God that brings us food," said one. "A farmer," said another, "because they grow the turkeys." "It looks more like a policeman, and they protect us." "I think," said Lavinia, who was always so serious and final, "that it is supposed to be all the hands that help us, but Douglas could only draw one of them."

Mrs. Klein had almost forgotten Douglas in her pleasure at finding the class so responsive. When she had the others at work on their numbering, she bent over his desk and asked whose hand it was. Douglas mumbled, "It's yours, Teacher."

Then Mrs. Klein recalled that she had taken Douglas by the hand from time to time—she often did that with the children. But that it should have meant so much to Douglas.... Perhaps, she reflected, this was her Thanksgiving, and everybody's Thanksgiving. Not the material things given unto us, but the chance in whatever small way to give something to others.

—Editorial in Baltimore *Sun*

CREATIVITY
the expression of inspired thought—resulting in some type of art form, e.g., poetry, painting, sculpture, or floral design. Creativity is that intellectual quality peculiar to man—his search for identity, personal freedom, satisfaction of accomplishment or fulfillment, resolved by his senses and reasoning. Man alone is endowed with these traits and talents which lead him into various fields of exploration, his avocation.

Science states the positive—factual, clinical, rational. Creativity, with intuition, is its opposite; it knows by a feeling, an inner voice and a compulsion to act.

Creative thought may lie dormant for a long time, but at the right time design evolves. Experiences stored in the subconscious mind spring forth, causing action. The idea, and the desire to create, develops itself into recognizable form—design. Creativity is spontaneous and varies with the individual's experience. It may even be a hidden talent of which we are unaware. Every person has an innate appreciation of the beautiful; it is motivation, energy and experience which distinguishes the individual.

The creative person holds on to his ideas and gives them play. He pays attention to vague feelings which are sometimes questioned by the pragmatic person. He will have a deep, broad and flexible awareness of himself. He will refuse to be content with established habits of perception, and be willing to break with custom—the hypnotic spell of tradition. He will be dedicated to work, to explore; he will not be content with the already established idea. A creative person is endowed with keen insight—knowledge without rational processes. He is more prone to venture into new, untested fields with a high degree of curiosity and unconventionality of thought.

Creative art may be considered an expression of man's spiritual being. It is a force that must find expression in a medium. It is more than a technical or mechanical skill with paints, clay, stone or plant materials. It is a natural inner force stemming from a basic desire for self-expression and freedom. Art (design) is emotion, imagination, vision where form takes shape. It is culminated through a medium in rhythmic harmony of basic principles (order). As life is motion similar to a growing plant, so is art. It is motion and must progress. It is evolution in rhythmic form. Static form dies. Floral art must move to unlimited horizons and integrate itself with the time to prevent stagnation.

This sensitive appreciation for creativeness is best expressed by the Persian poet Muslih Saadi, a Mohammedan sheik who lived about the 13th century, in his quatrain concerning two loaves of bread:

"If of thy mortal goods thou art bereft
And from thy slender store two loaves alone to thee are left
Sell one, and with the dole
Buy hyacinths to feed thy soul."

It is the feeding of the Soul (spiritual thinking) that illumines the imagination, creates and evolves functional form. This results in each civilization leaving its visual record. The body needs food for sustenance. The mind must have visions, imagination, for creativeness.

The creative process embodies tension, striving between positive and negative. This is the Yang-Yin of Chinese philosophy—intellect versus intuition, the conscious versus sub-conscious, conventional versus unconventional, complexity versus simplicity. It is a learning process by experimentation. It is willingness to venture forth, being forced by an inner urge of expression to produce. It is a force that must be reckoned with, be satisfied, be fulfilled. The end is never in sight, but, step by step, the ultimate goal is gained. When accomplished, it moves off to new fields, searching new horizons, new challenges, knowing that beyond there is more to be discovered.

Creativity is that never ending process exploring one's field to the fullest. It is progress.

As in the flower,
so the Soul of man ------ Universal order

ENTITY

The memory of this pair of sculptured hands emerged from the subconcious mind, revealing a message of entity of a world in their grasp — man's appeal to the spiritual.

This exquisite blossom (Monstera deliciosa) expresses fulfillment, being, the culmination of purpose — symbolic of man attuned to nature. The white corolla encases the spadix in perfect harmony with nature. The hands embrace this blossom — design evolved. Each has similar sculptural qualities in form and texture. Color harmony manifests perfection in a monochromatic hue. The round cross-section of the black walnut tree, with its concentric rings creating rhythm, is symbolic of earth. The white, worn pebbles rest on the earth's surface, depicting the waves of the sea. The hands in cupped position hold the blossom in whose power is held the secret of life — the seed.

PLATE 5
Entity

ABSTRACT FLORAL DESIGN

Rapid advances in social sciences, industrial environment, manner of thinking and living have brought about many changes to our way of life. Society is becoming more mature and complex. With this maturity comes the ability to understand, to accept, and to use in daily living unbridled freedom of thought and expression.

Art changes, along with scientific advances, are producing a totally new culture. In any transition, much that is extreme and bizarre always appears, but inevitably there emerges from experimental stages excellent examples of stable art forms. Well defined trends and pure form, governed by basic principles of design, are forging into prominence.

Freedom of expression, currently evolving in floral art, is indicative of contemporary changes in other art forms, such as painting, sculpture, and architecture. The western trend in presentation is toward less conformity to rules of limitation, fashion, tradition, with simplification of materials, freedom from pressure, and international influences. Thus, a new style reflecting beauty, freshness of vigor, and force is recognizable. Floral art has reached a milestone marking its maturity. Floral design assumes a new, clear meaning.

What is the thinking behind this new trend?

It is awareness of one's own individuality and his freedom of full expression by choice of materials, i.e. pigment, fresh, dried, or artificial materials. It is breaking with the hypnotic power of tradition and rules of set design.

The 19th and 20th centuries, and the Space Age, introduced this new concept in design. Traditional and gravitational ties that limited creative art were broken. Man began to see the relationship of objects in space, totally unrelated by the vanishing point perspective. This monocular principle prevailed while man was confined to earth; however, in space and with speed this new concept evolved. Cezanne fathered the beginning of abstraction in painting; consequently, the various "isms" developed — Cubism, Impressionism, Fauvism, etc. Also credit is due Picasso and Bracque for their adventures into Cubism, and Einstein who formulated the theory of relativity.

The function of an artist is to help one see (understand) the work created — not to convince or change opinion; to open broader vistas, giving new meaning to the familiar; to increase one's awareness and appreciation of order (beauty) in the mundane.

One's sub-conscious mind impels him toward a result which has its justification solely in one's sense of right — firmness to function. A work of art depends upon the subconscious resources of the interpreter's mind (an accumulation of past experiences — organized). If the work of art depends so much on the subconscious resources of the investigator's mind, the far less tangible and less measureable qualities of design must still be subjected to instinctive, rather than rational control. These are certain constants — standards of rightness, based on the laws of relationships.

Basic design principles have evolved from the inherent psychological need and ability to organize and arrange. Because we are mechanically-oriented in this era, these principles remain constant. A floral design is created by applying these principles (elements) — unity, rhythm, focus, dominance, proportion (scale), balance, line, color, etc. They guided floral art in the past, and through their continued usage, have become set rules. Rules were necessary for growth and expansion, to teach the novice, and to point the way. They set a standard of excellence by which to judge artistic quality. Creative artists are governed by principles, not rules.

To provide a basis of understanding of this contemporary advanced art form, it is well to consider art forms of the past, particularly floral art, and trace their history to establish their position today. No pattern or design, as we understand the use of the word, was developed in western culture until the American Garden Club movement developed patterns, using line from the Oriental, combined with the mass bouquet arrangement of Europe.

This author, through the study and analyzation of the use of flowers, in American culture, perfected the theory of geometric design with illustrations in his textbook, FLOWERS: GEOMETRIC FORM.

Further study by the author resulted in release of the restriction of geometric patterns — thus, revolutionizing the American concept of design. This theory of free form was presented in his book, FLOWERS: FREE FORM-INTERPRETIVE DESIGN.

With the understanding of these basic principles and freedom of thought, the ultimate in development of floral art has emerged — ABSTRACT DESIGN.

Abstract design evolved through a series of progressive steps of traditional designs as outlined in the following:

Classic reflects perfect order, definite mathematical and geometric design;

Romantic is visionary, strongly emotional, passionate, dominated by beauty;

Realistic is a faithful reproduction of nature, photographic, objective, with one point perspective, seeing the world as it is — everyday themes;

Geometric was developed from geometric patterns (circle, triangle, cube, etc.);

Free Form-Interpretive Design is pure design which evolves its own concept, independent of preconceived patterns; intrinsic value expressed in aesthetic beauty; timeless, elegant, with unlimited imagination.

ABSTRACT is visionary, intuitive, reflecting essence of purity in rhythm; perfect harmony is demonstrated with beauty and style.

Beauty is abstract — spiritual. It cannot be defined. Beauty is that illusive aesthetic quality that varies with one's taste. It is relative, functional in form, and approaches the ultimate in perfection. Beauty cannot be judged—it must be perceived.

Style is transitory, the expression of a time or period; the outgrowth of preference of motif, fashion, and materials; a distinctive, characteristic mode of the execution of an art.

Abstract is concerned with form, color, texture, and rhythmic relationship to each element, rather than depicting detail; it is non-objective, it implies, and generalizes.

Abstract is achieved by the creation of design (pattern), form in space without the use of ordinary linear perspective; no lines converge at a focal point; there is no vanishing point. This design gives form to vision, expressing rhythm and emotion. Abstraction is the intellectual process, sensory perception, by which the mind withdraws an impression from an object of experience.

Understanding the word "abstract" should not be difficult for we experience the act of "abstracting" every day of our lives. Unless we are intellectual hermits, we cannot help but feel this active force in the world.

The degree to which abstractions evolve depends upon the imagination and interpretation of the individual; objects must be non-objectively viewed. In painting, geometric forms may be adjusted to create composition. The artist has the media of colored pigment and uses his element to produce his picture. The media is abstract form and remains abstract, until applied to represent an object. The artist can spread his paints, paint over paint, and develop non-realistic form.

The flower arranger must take natural forms and use them to develop his design free of the natural growing habits of plant life. He may start with objective material, the symbol of whose form remains fixed to past remembrances, and reshape it, or mass it, for form, color, and texture, in a non-realistic manner to achieve results. Or, he may choose material that is familiar, or even exotic and strange, and though it is used with great imagination, the recognized form remains.

Since this art is no longer hampered by set rules, arrangements can be approached with an open mind. Thus, true creative ability finds expression in the unfolding of ideas.

The repetitious use of one container and one flower arrangement in various designs is used by this author for comparison. Also, the same flowers may be re-designed in various containers to show imagination and their versatility. Art work requires involvement. Select a container that is unique, or a problem. Study its lines extended. How does it enclose volume? As a starting point, one may combine ordinary (commonplace) materials or even exotic ones. Let the materials make their demands. Once a branch or flower is placed, it will require, demand, or suggest another elsewhere to balance it. Some materials may be placed forward and others backward, creating play of texture, color, and size; the placement of the objects determines volume. Omit naturalistic tendency; see form only. A relationship will develop; a tension of positive space will require negative space to satisfy a sense of order (perfect accord); a new appreciation of the objects develops. Each element should bear a direct, or oppositional, harmonious relationship to the other. Should one object be moved, tension is destroyed, therefore, breaking the binding force — rhythm.

Create floral composition without reference to motif or theme. Therefore, the degree to which a design approaches pure abstraction depends upon the eye of the viewer (an individual's keen insight, experience, education, and skill), for the eye can only see what the mind understands.

"Obedience is here:
even the silent flowers
speak to the inmost ear"
Onitsura

Design — obedience to principle

DESIGN PRINCIPLES (elements)

"Rhodora! if the sages ask thee why
This charm is wasted on the marsh and sky,
Tell them, dear, that if eyes were made for seeing,
*Then beauty is its own excuse for being."**

— Ralph Waldo Emerson

*Note: "Rhodora" (Rhododendron canadensis).

PLATE 6
Nijinsky—Rodin

PLATE 7
Wisteria Branch I

ABSTRACT

imagination — gives form to ideas — reflects the essence of purity in rhythm. In music, it is measured sound in time; in the dance, it is measured rhythmic movement; in flower arrangement, and all visual arts, it is rhythmic form in space.

This wisteria branch, sculptured by nature's forces, illustrates motion, grace, and rhythm — completeness standing alone. Its lines create the illusion of a ballet dancer whose inherent qualities cause the mind's eye to wander — to dance. The swift movements are repeated, like leaves floating in the breeze, and are meaningful to its form. Likewise, the lines of motion, creating rhythm in the statue of Nijinsky, are correlated.

PLATE 8
Wisteria Branch II

PLATE 11
Ballet Dancer—Sketch I

PLATE 9 Wisteria III
Grand Reverence

The rhythmic lines of the wisteria branch are expressive of ballet movements. This branch may be spiralling upright, or positioned in complete repose, presenting a sculptural effect. Regardless of how it is viewed, it relates to a movement of the dance.

PLATE 12
Ballet Dancer—Sketch II

PLATE 10
Wisteria Branch IV

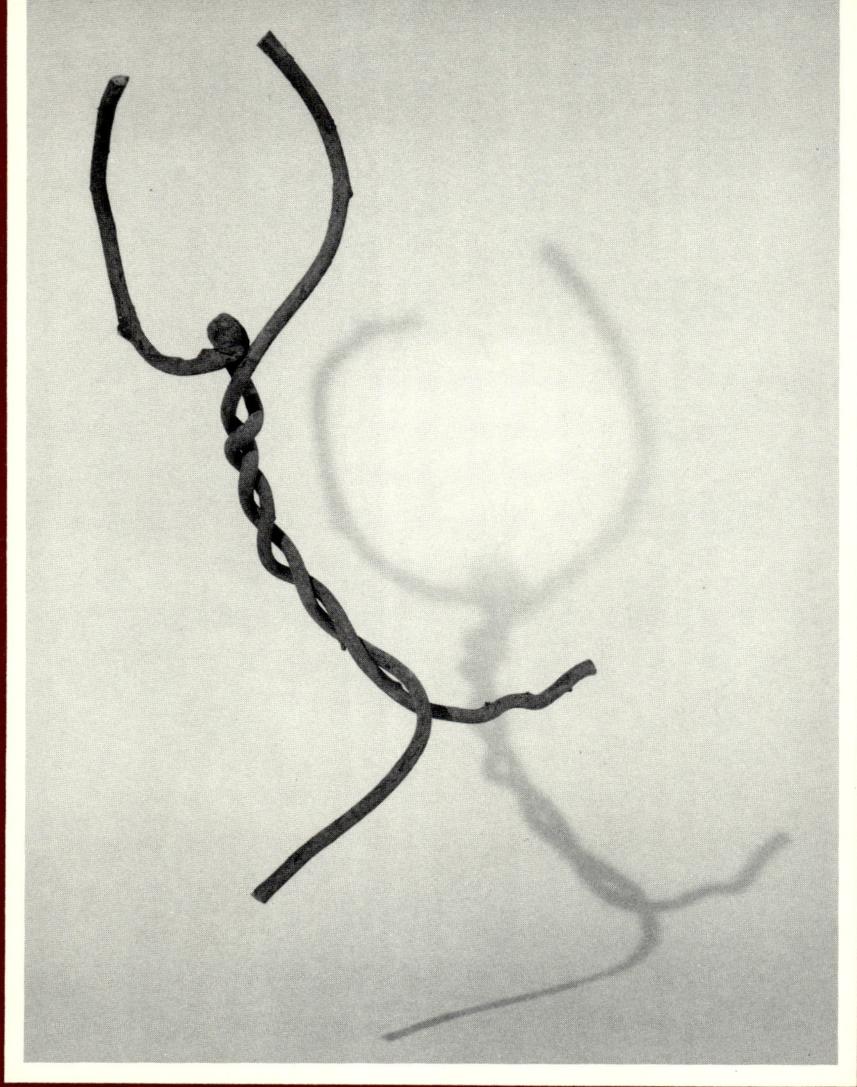

PLATE 13
Grand Jeté

In the Spring of 1912, Nijinsky, the great Russian ballet dancer, performed the ballet "The Afternoon of a Faun". Auguste Rene' Rodin, the sculptor, was so greatly enthralled by Nijinsky's capricious, powerful movements that he desired to capture this beauty in sculpture. (Plate 13)

Although this statue is unfinished, Rodin shows the strong, muscular characteristics of form in action, expressing rhythm, line, poise and balance.
The lines of the dancer and the branch abstract the ballet in perfect rhythm and harmony—a joyous correlation.

PLATE 14
Nijinsky—Rodin

PLATE 15
Ballet—Magnolia

BALLET — MAGNOLIA

This free form, crudely modeled, container has the same textural quality as the statue. Its twin openings accommodate the use of the wisteria branch which requires its mate, the beautiful Magnolia Soulangeana, to complete the design. Even though this flower still clings to its natural form, it becomes a vital companion to the sculptured wisteria which symbolizes the dancer — Nijinsky.

Principle of Unity

(composition, harmony) — each pattern is conceived as a whole and all of its elements are controlled by the relationship to each other which create harmony. There is dominance of the single motif, theme, or mood in the development of these compositions. Unity in the diverse forms expresses beauty and sensual joy in the transitory art of flower arrangement.

PLATE 17
"Rebosa"

REBOSA — SEAMAN

The bronze statue, "Rebosa," by Bonnie Seaman, is closely related to the flower arrangement, but in poised form. Her arms encircle space — defining volume — a void comparable to the void in the flower arrangement. The flowing lines are similar in each piece.

ADAGIO — PAS DE DEUX

The principals of the ballet are representative of the bleached sunflower seed pods. A movement of action in the dance is halted momentarily when the dancer holds his partner suspended in space. This swift movement is traced in the gracefully curved branch that extends into infinity.

The two tulips which are encircled, suggest the mood of the choreography, and speak of beauty in their final pose. The rhythmic motion is the primary element in this composition.

PLATE 16
Adagio—Pas de Deux

PLATE 18
Serenity

SERENITY

This Rosenthal free form ceramic figure speaks of a veiled woman in silent repose, contemplating the purity of the camellia blossom and plum branch in spiritual offering. Abstract line etches the form of the human figure.

TWO MADONNAS

Note the resemblance in form of the two figurines in Plate 18: The wooden one was carved by a native of Brazil, a primitive form spiritually inspired; the ceramic figure by Rosenthal of Germany has this same inspiration. All three forms are sympathetic in design.

PLATE 19
Two Madonnas

PLATE 20
High On A Windy Hil

PLATE 21
Rhythm In Curves

RHYTHM IN CURVES

The rings of the container are repeated in the undulating curves of the inverted royal poinciana seed pods. The round form of the camellia blossom is used as an abstract disc, stabilizing the pattern of the curves and tying the composition together.

HIGH ON A WINDY HILL

This figure is draped with a cloak which swirls with the wind, forming dominant lines. The illusion of dominance, a strong force, expresses the intrinsic value of the composition.

The container, an electric power line insulator, receives a bolt of lightning through the inverted royal poinciana seed pods, then bursting into a flash of color through the strelitzia — energy is dissipated.

Principle of Line____

is beauty in itself. It is direction. Line is the visual path the eye follows, producing motion, defining volume, areas, and planes, thus providing the skeletal pattern. Its inherent qualities appeal to one's senses and reason, satisfying the aesthetic taste.

It may be severe and masculine, exhibiting strength and vitality; or, it may be dainty and feminine, expressing gentleness.

Line is never static; it produces a vibrant quality, giving movement and life to design.

Periods of history are identified by line; e.g. the Rococo style flourished with linear forms. Contemporary line "form" assumes a new meaning of great impact. It is envisioned in tri-dimensional manner.

Paul Klee, referring to his drawing, "The Mocker Mocked," 1930, Museum of Modern Art, said that "he wanted to take a walk with a line." His drawing is line enclosing volume; its overlapping and reverse curves suggest depth. The outline of a face appears in caricature, because of the peculiarity of the human mind and its training of extracting recognizable features. However, this was not the intention of the artist.

The mind may refer to related objects, strange animals, faces, buildings, etc., which emerge unpredictably. Shapes may have an interesting relationship to each other, but not necessarily to the whole composition. Their outlines, intervals side to side, and front to back, are fascinating in themselves, but may result in non-representation to pure abstract forms.

The ceramic piece in the illustration is rhythm in linear form. Ceramic ribbon shapes volume and produces motion; and because of its black and white color combination, immediately suggests the image, "The Nun", Plate 21.

PLATE 21
The Nun

PLATE 23
The Nun With Lily

THE NUN WITH LILY

Since the imagery of "The Nun" is so clearly stated, her beauty is enhanced by the poised calla lily — associated symbolism of purity.

Similarity of curves, forms, colors, and textures is dramatically emphasized.

THE NUN WITH CRUCIFIX

The design is climaxed by the strong upswing of the green stem of the calla lily. A deep religious connotation is expressed by the addition of the primitive crucifix — pure abstraction results.

PLATE 24
The Nun With Crucifix

Every shape in nature can be abstracted into a geometric symbol. For example, flowers may be seen as basic art forms:

a sphere - dahlia, chrysanthemum;
a spike - delphinium, gladiolus;
a triangle - trillium, orchid;
a radial - dandelion, sunflower.

Geometric shapes speak to the floral artist in the same general way. A designer learns to see the abstract symbolic elements in the materials, and to use them as basic units in a design. It is the combination of these shapes which creates rhythm.

Think about a leaf or seed pod. Consider the natural shapes and how they may be *stylized;* enlarge upon their shapes, textures, and markings. The veining may be exaggerated to become even more decorative. Or, consider the round forms of the allium blossom or the dandelion seed pod; each shape is a variation of radiation. The eye must be trained to *abstract* the simplicity of shapes from complex geometric relationships.

PLATE 25
Natural Rock Forms

Natural rock formations Plates 24 and 25 relate to these pieces of art as shown in "Narcissus - Slave to Beauty", Plate 27, "The Nun", Plate 21, and specifically to "A Muse", 1917, Plate 26, by Constantin Brancusi. The rocks, suggestive of body forms, which were formed by nature and worn smooth by time, obliterate details of the human figure, as Brancusi did in his superb sculptured figure. He abstracted the metal to suggest a torso, eliminating all representational details. Yet, this highly polished piece is dignified, illusive, and demanding in feeling. It is an experience — leaving much to the imagination.

PLATE 26
Natural Rock Forms

A MUSE — CONSTANTIN BRANCUSI, 1917

Why this relationship to flower arrangement? It helps one see form in its natural state — to create design from material at hand — to relate. It is easy to compare flower arrangements to sculpture because of the tri-dimensional factors.

PLATE 27
A Muse

Courtesy of...The Museum of Fine Arts...Houston, Texas

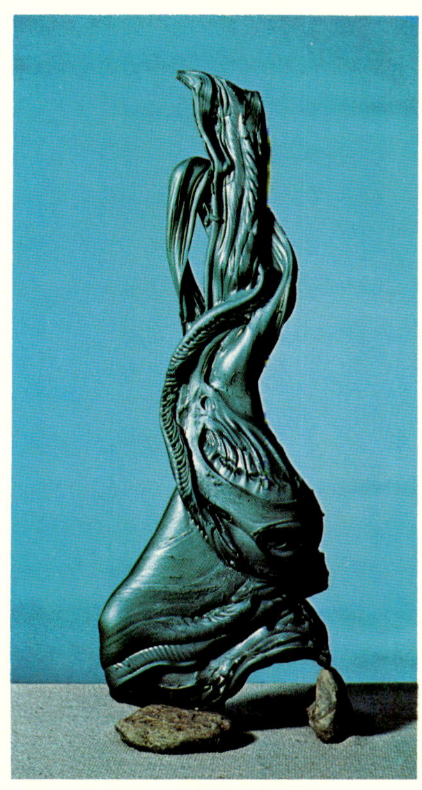

PLATE 29
Flamenco Dancer

FLAMENCO DANCER

Discarded plastic materials from a manufacturing plant are used because of their interesting shapes. This abstract figure resembles the form of a kneeling figure. The lines and folds appear to be a mantilla draping the body.

SLAVE TO BEAUTY

The white ceramic figure appears to be admiring her beauty in a mirror, or combing her hair. Daffodil blossoms have been contrived in modulated sequence to express her narcissus complex. One-half of an aspidistra leaf simulates the mirror. The bleached wisteria vine relates to her form. Floral material is complementary to the design. This figure is similar in form to the dancer (Plate 28).

PLATE 28
Slave To Beauty

PLATE 30
Easter Morn

EASTER MORN

The crucifix, by the sculptor William S. McKenzie, is an assemblage of welded iron pieces. Brilliant yellow flowers remind one of the sun that has arisen, promising continuity of life. The red blossoms and green leaf emphasize the vibrancy of life.

An entirely different mood and theme are presented by changing accessory materials, giving play to the imagination — creativity.

PLATE 31
Twin Daffodils

TWIN DAFFODILS

The designer of this container gave distinction to an ordinary shape by the radiating medallion of hemp twine. The orange disc is woven onto the radiating spokes of twine. Two daffodils, whose trumpets have been divided into segments, form the abstract flowers and repeat the radiation.

The composite flower of contrived daffodils, forms a cone which is encircled by red anthurium, adds contrasting color interest to the composition. The white branch synchronizes the two designs and defines the pictorial space.

Principle of Radiation ____

is dispersion, divergence, a cosmic force which illuminates, and vibrates. It is expressed by rhythmic harmony in a sequence of elements originating from a central point of origin.

In nature radial lines form many patterns. Concentric circles appear when a pebble is dropped into a quiet pool; the sun's rays radiate from a central point; this identical form is seen in the dandelion and allium blossoms. However, in the sunflower and nautilus shell, the lines radiate outwardly in a spiralling motion (Plate 38).

UNTITLED (1964) — TADASKY

The Japanese artist, Tadasky, in his painting (untitled 1964) created an optical illusion by drawing circular lines in pulsating motion. They are carefully graded in widths to create dynamic tension that moves forward and backward, similar to kinetic art.

Courtesy of...The Museum of Fine Arts...Houston, Texas

PLATE 32
Untitled (1964)—Tadasky

PLATE 34
Samoan Yucca

SAMOAN YUCCA

In Western Samoa, on the opposite side of the world, this same desire to decorate is exemplified by using hibiscus blossoms on each point of the yucca, and crowning the plant with plumeria (frangipani) flowers. It is interesting to note that two diverse cultures would produce the same result.

ST. JOHN'S YUCCA

The primitive urge to design, to embellish, to create beauty, is innate in all peoples and must be expressed in some form.

In the West Indies this yucca plant, with its radiating pointed leaves, inspired someone to decorate it with egg shells. A festive mood is created.

This pattern relates closely to the allium Page 64, Plates 35-37.

PLATE 33
St. John's Yucca

PLATE 35
Allium

ALLIUM
Allium blossoms disperse filaments from the apex of their stems in rhythmic harmony.

PLATE 36
WAR MEMORIAL—AUSTRALIA

EL ALAMEIN—gift from the United States

WAR MEMORIAL — AUSTRALIA
The war memorial fountain in Sydney, Australia, is another beautiful illustration of radial design. A horizontal spray of water is dispersed from each filament. The design is comparable to the salsify seed pods in Plates 72 and 73. Man again returns to nature for inspiration.

PLATE 37
Metal Flowers—Bartoia

METAL FLOWERS — BARTOIA

These fountains fashioned of metal rods resemble the radial filaments of allium and dandelion seed pods. The simplicity of form is so related to nature that fields of flowers dance upon the mind's eye, reminiscent of joyous experiences. Pure beauty is created by repetitious forms. (Kodak exhibit, World's Fair, N.Y.)

BIRDS IN FLIGHT FORMATION

Birds in flight formation create an abstract radial pattern. The fluttering strokes and brilliant color of their wings show the element of surprise. The lower circle of birds has just been flushed from its resting place. The line of motion is directed upward by the foliage, uniting the flocks.

PLATE 38
Bird In Flight Formation

Principle of Contrast____

a governing principle in all art. There is pleasing movement in the juxtaposition of materials, for the eye is forced to examine each form; positive and negative vie for interest.

BOLD STATEMENT

Bold statements are made with this beautiful Arnau vase — so perfect it stands alone to be admired. Its radiating segments are visually controlled by the focal point (a void). Distinction is achieved by exposing the radial divisions in the top half of its circular form. The mind's eye fills in the remainder of the sphere. The lower portion being enclosed, tells one that it was meant to be a vase.

Horizontal lines of the banksia and the Chinese junk call attention to the horizontal division of the vase. The interesting curves of the vine and other forms cause the eye to visualize fascinating images.

The Chinese junk is propelled by the palm fronds, and directed by a swamp banksia (B. littoralis) which is related to the Proteaceae family. Two Fuji chrysanthemums blend in form and texture.

PLATE 39
Bold Statement

RADIAL INFINITY

The radial design formed in the container has a bull's-eye focus which holds the eye at first viewing. However, the opposing forces in the intriguing materials equate the dominance of this one point focus. The equation of interest is keenly felt, because of the vibrant tension created between the units.

The cup-shaped protea blossoms (P. neriifolia) emphasize the shape of the solid portion of the vase, and accent the horizontal lines which oppose the strong vertical lines.

The long left-hand palm frond carries the eye to the horizontal plane of the top protea, ending abruptly against the aspiring terminal leaf. This plane intensifies the horizontal line of the container and lower blossom. The 90 degree angle thus formed corresponds to the similar angle formed by the lower flower and palm stem; parallelism is developed, giving distinction to the entire composition. Should this upper blossom be extended beyond the tip of this frond, the line would carry the eye to the apex thus following a traditional tendency of design.

The radial palm fronds with their stems give strong directional force, further equating the interest and value of each unit.

PLATE 41
Radial Infinity

Principle of Focus

(Center of Interest) — directs the attention. In traditional geometric design, it is the point of origin or convergence to which the eye is directed by virtue of monocular perspective. It is emphasized by the strongest color, and the most fully developed blossom (Plate 42). All other units are in subordination. In Free Form-Interpretive Design and Abstract, an entirely different concept of focus is presented; the one point perspective is eliminated.

In these designs the relationship of elements fulfills requirements of design. By juxtaposition of each piece of material, in form and color, the design is coordinated in opposing rhythmic force in space, pleasing our sense of order. A new experience is felt; space assumes a new importance; interest is equated (Plate 41).

PLATE 42
Radiating Forms I—GALAX ROSE

RADIATING FORMS I — GALAX ROSE

The galax rose ties the unrelated units into a pleasing arrangement of contrasting textures, colors, and forms. The beautiful twisted vine, which forms an abstract figure, encloses the artichoke blossom whose petals also repeat the radiating form. The yellow triangular flowers are oven-baked yucca (Spanish dagger) leaves, which are grouped around a black-eyed susan pod.

PLATE 43
Radiating Forms II

RADIATING FORMS II

The Arnau vase is used as the central feature, and acts as a perpendicular opposing force. The petals of the roses and the galax rosette repeat the radial design of the vase.

Bursting, radiating lines of the dried palm leaf originate from the galax rose.

PLATE 44
Triangular Form

TRIANGULAR FORM

This traditional geometric design of roses and nerine lilies was used as a counterbalance. The undulating, radiating lines from the rose at the focal point flow into the graceful Balinese figure.

PLATE 45
Abstract—Interplay I

ABSTRACT — INTERPLAY I

The strong masculine line of plastic entwines the container with the bold statement of the aspiring primitive sword — cutting space, dividing volume, defining pattern, and encircling the beautiful man-made "flower".

The eye is compelled to move from one point to another with interest. The forms are simple, carefully balanced, both physically and dynamically. Each unit expresses a vitality in itself. Textures are in direct opposition, yet complementary by their contrasts.

This "flower" is the result of the imagination—
abstract
man-made
contrived
It is made from the seed sheaths of the Japanese varnish tree (Firmiana simplex). The "calyx" is painted black and the "petals" a brilliant orange. These materials are arranged to simulate a natural flower. This assemblage is decorative, impelling, and provacative in color, line, and form.

PLATE 46
Abstract—Interplay I (Detail)

PLATE 47
Abstract Interplay

ABSTRACT INTERPLAY II

Additional skeletal herring-bone strelitzia leaves (Strelitzia Reginae) add direction and interest, changing the design to a different composition, but keeping the essence of abstract.

Strong silhouette value is exemplified in each segment of the design. The interplay of shapes — the flanges, a positive force — is repeated in the negative spaces of the ribbed foliage. Semaphore signals are defined in this foliage which accent the simulated "blossom" at their intersection. Further movement is traced in the plastic, which forces the eye to travel from segment to segment.

ABSTRACT INTERPLAY III

Strelitzia blosoms have replaced the plastic and simulated "blossom", producing a semi-abstract design of a pleasing vertical composition. There is strong opposition to this vertical line which is opposed by the horizontal planes of the flanges of the vase, and the horizontal skelotonized leaf. The two lower strelitzia blossoms reinforce the horizontal plane.

PLATE 48
Abstract Interplay III

POISED BIRD

This orange-black ceramic bird has simulated wings of strelitzia foliage, which was abstracted to suggest the pinions of the bird. There is a wedding of plant materials and container, producing a rare relationship which complements each segment. The principles of Cubism are reflected in this design.

PLATE 49
Poised Bird

BIRD IN FLIGHT

This design is in direct opposition to Plate 49. Its wings suggest motion and show varied positions (in accord with principles established in Cubism, which are obtained by the flattening and superimposing of planes, and the polyhedral fragmentation of volumes).

PLATE 50
Bird In Flight

PLATE 51
Round—Square

ROUND — SQUARE

The four strelitzia blossoms form a square in the round vase. These blossoms point inward toward the apex of the central axis. One-half of each strelitzia leaf has been fenestrated in abstract form to maintain the open area. The other half of each leaf was left natural to solidify the pattern.

PLATE 52
Blue Parabola

BLUE PARABOLA

The contemporary blue crystal bowl gives freedom of choice in design. It is provocative and challenging in its demands to remain free. Its intrinsic value must be preserved and enhanced. Any material which would destroy its lines or compete with color would infringe on its value.

The shape of the leaves and placement follow the curvature of the bowl. The parabolic curves originate from the locus, at the point of the directrix. The light blue color of the lower portion of the bowl directs the eye upward from point to point and outward.

To dramatize quality, a simulated hyacinth blossom of carnations was added. The contrast in color and fine texture is complementary.

RHYTHM IN ORANGE

After materials are assembled, each piece demands its own right of placement. The imagination is aglow — ideas rush through one's mind; design is formed by his own intuitions.

The ancient altar bronze, used for *rikka* arrangements, is from a Buddhist temple. It expresses strength, and holds the rhythmic, orange, entangled rods in elegance. This composition satisfies the aesthetic taste.

Brilliant orange dahlias, disc-shaped with radiating petals, fill the requirements of a floral motif that blends with the curves of the altar piece. The secondary container is subdued, but its shape curves with undulating rhythm to speak for itself. It does not compete with its bronze counterpart. The petals of the flowers are in perfect order, radiating from their central axis; whereas, the plastic rods are massed in confusion in the focal area, but extend outward in rhythmic, curvilinear lines.

PLATE 53
Rhythm In Oran

SENTINEL

The illusion of drama, the dance, the opera, and fascinating stories are conjured up in this fantastic assemblage of roots and plant growth. These are heavily painted with numerous coats of bronze which establish the pattern. They cut, fill, and demand space to such a degree that with or without floral material the design is sculptural, nonobjective, and pleasing to the eye. Eleagnus, weeping willow, or supple spring growth, are excellent plant materials for this configuration. Foiliage placed in semaphore fashion accents the vertical and horizontal lines. A perfect blossom of strong color and solid form stabilizes the movement.

PLATE 54
Sentinel

PLATE 55
Sunset Sails

PLATE 56
"Regatta"

REGATTA

In this piece of welded sculpture, "Regatta", by Reg Coghlan, the shapes of sail boats are recalled with multi-colors cutting the breeze. The crosses represent the reflections on the Mediterranean Sea. The shapes and colors in these two pieces are correlated.

SUNSET SAILS

Color and line are the dominant features in this Italian container. They make their demands. The blue is reminiscent of the Mediterranean Sea, and the orange verticals of the descending sun. Foliage has been cut to represent sails. Tangerine carnations, which have been deftly fashioned into a composite flower, are used for color and texture.

FELUCCA

The impressions of one's travels linger in the memory to fulfill their mission when the right time permits. The Nile delta, with its ancient history, is romantic and reminiscent of the feluccas which have sailed the river for a millennium. These boats were made of reeds and had sails of cloth.

The triangular shape of these boats has a special mythological meaning in this area, as seen in the shape of the pyramids. This contemporary container, which is true in color and texture, is used as a stylized felucca. One leaf (Chamadorea elegans) has been trimmed to suggest the sail and complete the triangle. Carnations represent the boatmen who are active and alert. Earthy tones of container and flowers are representative of Egypt. Motion is implied in both foliage, sailing in the breeze, and in the flange forming the prow of the boat. The Mediterranean blue sky is a compatible background.

PLATE 57
Felucca

PARENTHESIS I

An antique Japanese usabata, which rises high above the water, holds pine cone ginger (Zingiber zerumbet). These cones are accented with the careful use of abstract aspidistra leaves. One leaf has been trimmed to demand attention; the lower one rolled to harmonize with the base.

PLATE 58
Parenthesis I

PLATE 59
Parenthesis II

PARENTHESIS II

Nerine lilies stand at attention and march upon the scene. Their shapes repeat the filigree work of the base of the container which represents ocean waves.

PLATE 60
Parenthesis III

PARENTHESIS III

This abstract design complements the contemporary vase. Its crescent shape is repeated by two, long, narrow croton leaves, which were wired and shaped to reiterate the cupped pattern. A skeletonized prickly pear blade (Opuntia compressa) opens its double veining form, which encases the carnation blossom, and solidifies the composition. The carnation is used for color, texture, and form.

PLATE 61
Parenthesis IV

PARENTHESIS IV

The striking main flower, Curcuma leuchoriza, is demanding in its exotic qualities and must be accented. Its rarity forces the designer to acknowledge its beauty. Each elliptical petal shape of this dominant flower is enhanced by the repeated shape of the lily petals. The curcuma is used in its natural form, establishing a central axis as an exclamation point; however, the white lilies have been used in an abstract form to contrast and give emphasis. Using the lily petals in this abstract manner gives new dimension and interest to the design.

PLATE 62
Parenthesis V

PARENTHESIS V

Variegated aspidistra leaves give strength and vitality to the design. They reinforce the suggested lines established by the lilies, which enclose volume containing the curcuma blossom.

The curves in each lily petal are repeated by the curves of the aspidistra leaves and the legs of the Oriental table.

PLATE 63
Carolina Vase I

PLATE 64
Carolina Vase II

CAROLINA VASE I

The ceramic artist gave distinction to this simple vertical form by adding elliptical flanges midway up the vase. Line foliage positioned in pairs, back to back, and placed in a vertical position, accents height.

CAROLINA VASE II

In this variation, the foliage is bent horizontally to complement the center of interest of the vase, the flanges. Horizontal lines are emphasized, rather than the vertical line, which give distinction to the composition. Strong floral accent is given in the abstract column of tangerine carnations.

PLATE 65
Love Story

LOVE STORY

Two allium flowers escape their foe who is poised to strike from its place on the table. The swift, curved motion of this blossom is restated in the curved leaf which traces the elopement. Distinction is achieved by the green curved leaf entwining the two blossoms in a protective manner. A pleasing proportion is established by the curved leaf, equally dividing the composition into three parts — the height of the container, green stems, and blossoms.

ABSTRACT #101 — FLORIDA

An interesting juxtaposition of unrelated materials — allium, shell, and flower — tells a story of the sea shore. Each unit is so closely related to its neighbor that the slightest movement of one or the other would destroy the tension that holds this piece in perfect rhythm. The graceful shape of the conch shell, with its curves ending in infinity, sets the spiralling motion. This motion is immediately transposed to the allium stem which ends in its round blossom. The camellia blossom repeats the round form of the allium, while its single leaf points upward with the shell. The base is a cross-section of a walnut tree which gives stability to the rhythmic motion and dominance to the round forms.

PLATE 66
Abstract #101—Florida

PLATE 67
Ruffled Feathers

PLATE 68
French Bird I

PLATE 69
French Bird II

FRENCH BIRD I

In this French bird, the tall bamboo root is an abstraction of this piece. It is expressive of the rhythm, form, and texture of the bird. The protea (P. lutens) adds floral interest and harmony.

FRENCH BIRD II

Simulated wings of opuntia leaves (skelentonized) are added to the bamboo root to indicate flight in the manner of Cubism. A bird-of-paradise blossom restates the image of the ceramic bird — each being an illusive abstraction.

RUFFLED FEATHERS

This ceramic abstraction is by the French artist, Jean Dureal. Its interest lies in its unusual shape and stylized wing design.

The forward placement of the rolled aspidistra leaves emphasizes the beak and eye of the bird. The upright pair of leaves simulates the crest, while the third pair (tail feathers) creates the opposing force of Yang-Yin, and rotates in opposite directions.

Texture is emphasized by the pin-cushion protea, and is in sympathy with the abstract wing design.

RELATED FORMS—BIRDS

Abstract is visionary. It implies, generalizes rather than depicting detail. Abstract is concerned with form, color, texture and rhythmic relationship of each element. So with this creative floral arrangement, the power of suggestion fires the imagination.

The mind is forced to identify the "bird" form in both the ceramic pot and the bird-of-paradise, an illusion by association. Imagination gives form to ideas reflecting the essence of purity in the rhythmic lines which are continuous in each element. Line, mass, and color are carefully interplayed. So continuous is the movement from one unit to another that ecstatic pleasure becomes its finest quality. The half strelitzia leaf, whose veins are prominent, expresses the pinions of the bird. It is a rare instance when the combination of materials are so closely united.

PLATE 70
Related Forms—Birds

PLATE 71
Green Cobra

GREEN COBRA

Simple forms are combined in a vertical line to emphasize their pointed incurved shapes. There is dominance of a single motif (the alerted cobra).

The chartreuse bowl of fine texture holds its foliage whose points depict the hood of a cobra. The auratum lily petals have been formed in abstract design to emphasize this motif. At the base, orange flowers are massed for weight, texture, and contrast.

PLATE 72
Objective Moon

OBJECTIVE—MOON

The theme of this design expresses the space age—imagination exploding. The space capsule, a white crystal vase, has been launched from its pad, piercing the sky with a terrific impact as expressed in the telescoped lily petals. The fire of the explosion is represented by croton foliage at the base. Excitement and motion take the mind on its journey to the moon.

PLATE 73
Balinese Pagoda

PLATE 74
Room Setting—Pagoda

ROOM SETTING — PAGODA

This arrangement blends perfectly into a modern living room setting. The lamp is contemporary, yet oriental in character. The figurine is Balinese — a primitive, stylized carving of teakwood. Its graceful lines express the rhythmic pulsation of their daily life. Each detail in the carving, in the flower arrangement, and in the lamp is characteristic of the curvature in their architecture. These curves are opposed by the cubical form of the contemporary chair.

BALINESE PAGODA

The Balinese dancers curve their fingers similarly to the ornamentations of the temple roofs. Croton foliage is curved in a like manner. Lily petals are telescoped into an abstract tower to simulate pagoda temples which capture the essence of Bali.

GRECIAN HORSE

The original of this cast is artistically one of the most important single objects in the classical collection of the Metropolitan Museum of Art. The modeling has just that combination of realism and stylization with which Greek art, of the first half of the 5th century, achieved its unsurpassed triumphs. The rendering of the mouth suggests that it was being pulled by a bridle. The glories of Grecian history are embodied in the stately carriage of this horse. The clean cut, bold definite form is contemporary. The abstract flower arrangement is the perfect tribute to this great piece of art. The golden allium blossoms reproduce the body lines of the statuette. Lilies, perfect in structural form, are symbolic of the Olympic torch. The bold, textured container is a stylized chalice. Rarely does one find materials that complement each other to such a high degree.

PLATE 75
Grecian Horse

Principle of Rhythm ____

is the measured harmonious relationship between mass, line, form, and color — the binding force that satisfies; it is vital to design. It is achieved by continuity of line, movement without monotony, repetition of materials with variation of color, gradation of sizes, and dominance of a single motif.

PLATE 76
Yang-Yin

YANG-YIN

The rhythmic forms of Yang-Yin, bronze sculptures by Bonnie Seaman, entwine their arms in embrace, creating a rhythmic force that binds the two as one unit. These fulfill the Chinese philosophy denoting masculine and feminine forms, positive and negative qualities, active forces in nature—completeness.

ALLIUM

Allium stems (A. mutabile) also, produce this rhythmic interplay which show their close relationship to Yang-Yin philosophy (Plate 76).

PLATE 77
Allium

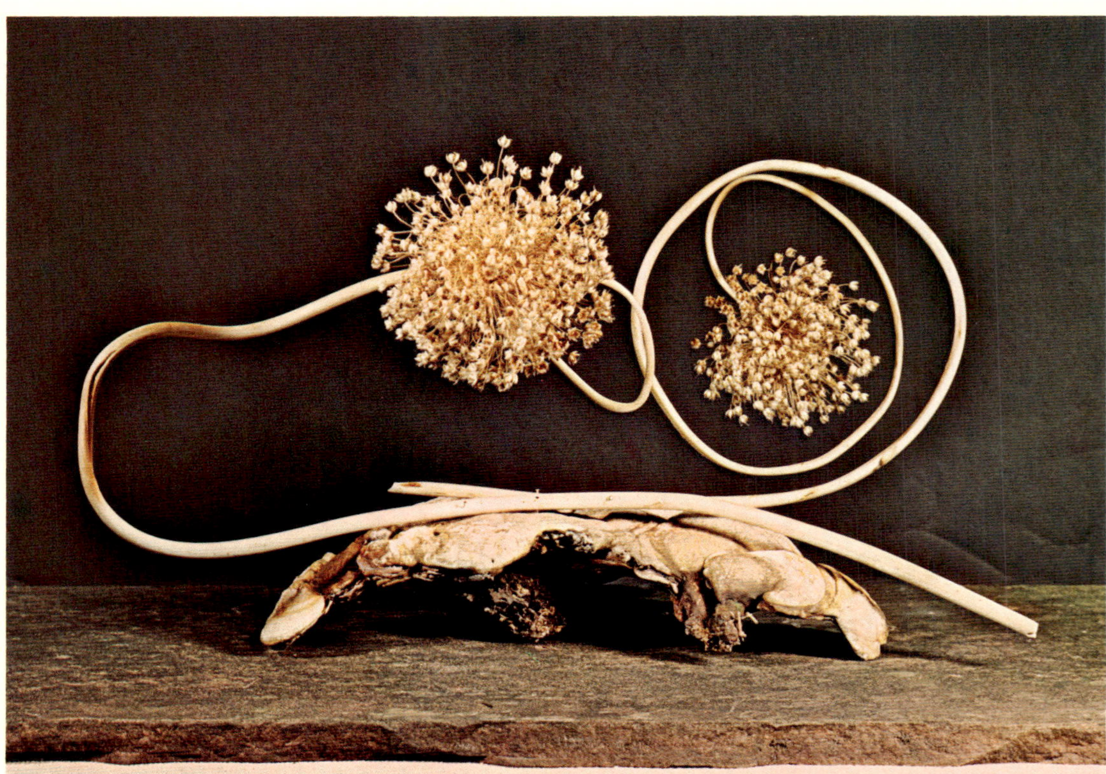

PLATE 78
Autumn Play

AUTUMN PLAY

The undulating allium stems enclose the circular, vertical fungi, then rise like musical chords. Their graceful, melodic, syncopated movements, drifting slowly over a horizontal fungi base, increase in rhythm then abruptly stop in a clash of radiation. This movement is playful. It is pleasing to the eye and the ear for it leads one to visualize an experience — a musical drama — a symphony of "eye sound". Salsify (Targopogon parrifolius) seed pod stems glide from this base; their lines continue a smooth outward motion like musical notes into space. The swerving lines of the bark of the ponderosa pine tree formation, worn by time and shaped by wind, reinforce this swirling movement and float into the autumn breeze.

Dried elements in these designs tell of seasons past when they, too, danced in the morning's dew; now they are preserved in their permanency as sculptured forms.

DAWN

— a nymph gently moves upon the cosmic scene, expressing quiet solitude of everlasting beauty. This graceful, dancing figure, "NUDE", was created by the contemporary sculptress, Virginia Morris Pollack, and is in the collection of the author.

PLATE 79
Dawn

"Time is the pod
that holds the seed
of every need
Created by God."
- *by Margie Lee Johnson*

POSITIVE AND NEGATIVE STATEMENTS

The etched, radiating design, encircling the void in the ceramic container, is also created in the woven raffia forms which are suspended one above the other. Their voids are negative statements, equalizing the two positive masses — allium seed pods. Their stems enclose volume which tie the composition together. The rhythmic interplay of positive and negative forces moves forward and backward, entwining each other in space. Suspension is a constructional force, adding a fascination of vibrant tension. The attention is held to this design by this force.

PLATE 80
Positive & Negative Statements

The square is basic in all art forms. Structurally, it appears in architecture, furniture, contemporary painting, etc.

In flower arrangement, it poses a problem because of its equal corners, each competing with the other. It is blunt, bold, and firm. However, a cross-section (the triangle), which creates unequal angles, is more relaxing and is associated with action and growth.

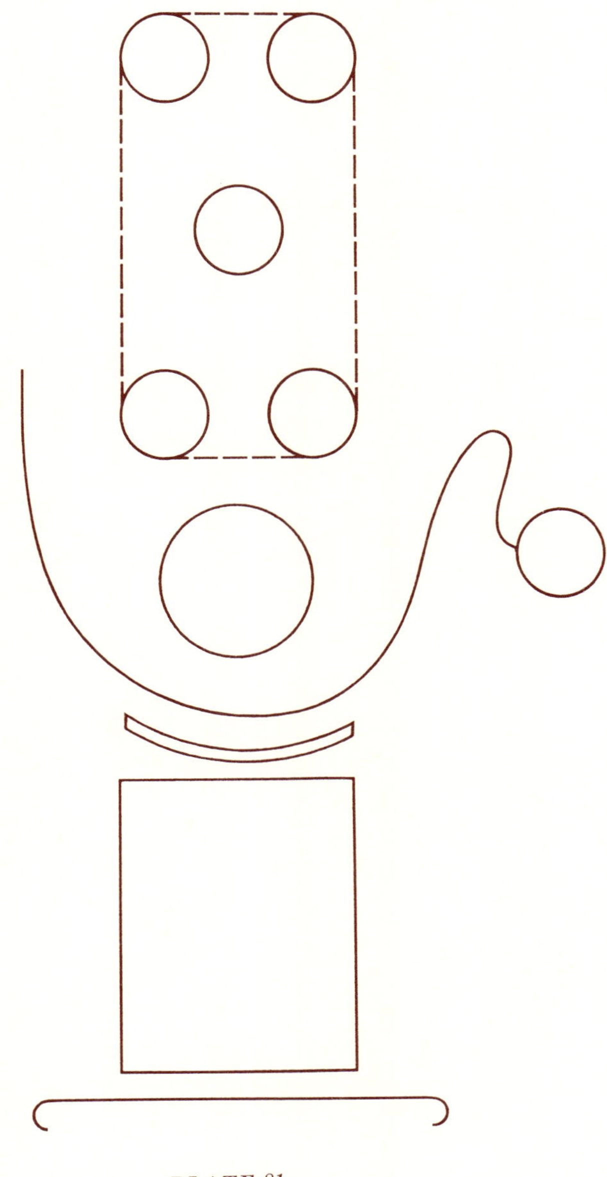

PLATE 81
Design Analysis

RED CAMELLIA

The curved flange of the square container is emphasized by the curved allium stem and round camellia blossom. The strong, parabolic curves of the flange and allium stem add dynamic force. These three circular lines divide the two rectangular forms. The outline described by the four allium blossoms repeats the shape of the rectangular container. The red camellia blossom makes its own statement and is related to the central allium head. The base adds emphasis to the lines that narrate design. Accents give variety and interplay to solids and voids, each equally important to the picture.

PLATE 82
Red Camelia

PLATE 83
The Blue Sphere

PLATE 84
(Figure)—2—MAKI

PLATE 85
Room Setting

THE BLUE SPHERE

In this geometric floral composition of rectangles and circles, each shape complements the other without competing. Each one demands attention, causing the eye to travel. The container makes a definite statement in its rectangular form, but suggests circular motion by the suspended flange. The curved allium stem encircles the fungi disc and terminates in the blue sphere. This curve and sphere complement the red crescent and blue disc in the picture. Note the relationship of pattern in the five circular discs of chair upholstery and five alliums. Shapes are held in bond by strong tension of opposing forces.

The Japanese block print by Haku Maki (Untitled), states the circular motion by the wide brush stroke enclosing the blue sphere. The rectangular form is suggested by vertical strokes which overlap, showing depth.

ROOM SETTING

Abstract forms are repeated in related abstract forms in the author's room setting. Harmony is created by each rectangular unit — the chair, the picture, and the complementary flower arrangement.

THE RED CARNATION

Using the basic forms of art, the square and the circle, a distinctive order of abstractions makes definite statements. This container is a work of art—an entity unto itself, a thing of beauty, which is vibrant and piques the

imagination. It is not static. The gradation of color from black to light gray, forces the upward movement through the abstracted foliage which is rectangular in form. The foliage is secured in the circular opening, which bisects the rectangular container. The herringbone pattern relieves the monotony, which gives originality and distinction to the arrangement. It is repetitious of the native bamboo fences so often seen in The Peoples Republic of China—the ultimate use of native materials which becomes a work of art. The eye follows a demanding path from dark to light; then on upward through the stem, terminating in the red circular carnation. This blossom complements the circular void of the container, which is the dominant feature of this ceramic piece.

PLATE 86
The Red Carnation

PLATE 87
Chinese Bamboo Fence

PLATE 88
The Red Carnatic
With Base

TRIANGLES AND CIRCLES

Geometric shapes of triangles and circles repeat themselves in sequence, forming a movement that is in friendly accord with each other. These allium blossoms may be arranged when fresh and allowed to dry in their natural shapes.

Triangular patterns are stated by the container. A similar triangular form is created by the crossed stems, and is also repeated in the triangular bunch of grapes. Round forms are seen in each grape and composite blossom. Rhythmic geometric forms of triangles and circles, with color interest, give this arrangement distinction and individuality. Volume is enclosed, producing negative spaces which are as important as the positive. The eye is forced to move from area to area with pleasure and confidence. The laws of relationship governing the principles, create harmony even with their opposing shapes. Each pattern is controlled by this relationship. There is dominance of forms in this composition.

PLATE 89
Line Analysis

PLATE 90—Triangle And Circle

DRAMATIC INVOLVEMENT

A work of art speaks to us in many different ways. It may be impelling or provocative — in either case there is reaction. If appealing, it will create ideas that picture a complete design — it will cause us to act — become involved and want to create. Thus, a work of art will give the student the opportunity to see for himself, and enjoy the work of art on his own terms.

Now, with a new approach, and with a new concept, one begins to create spontaneously, to see beauty in form just for the pleasure of its being. After having studied and practiced the true principles of any art form, one will recognize the intrinsic value of the character of the materials. It is only by a fuller understanding of them that one advances.

The sculptured, pink plastic curves, twists, moves in and out, cuts space, and defines volume. It is playful. It is busy. It is a challenging decorative form. There is push and pull of space and line. The eye cannot rest. One must free one's self of all inhibitions.

The subtle, but severe, straight lines of the sansevieria leaves are at right angles to each other, and are firmly held in place with the begonia leaf. This pattern is in direct opposition to the strong, scalene line of the curving plastic which encircles this foliage, merging two patterns into one. Anthurium blossoms, similar in shape, color, and floral pattern, further unite with the opposing forces. The blossoms become so involved in the design that they reinforce the scaline line of plastic. Yet, they restate the triangular pattern of a strongly suggested horizontal line parallel to the wooden base. These lines stress the equilibrium of forces which stabilize the design, while the eye is forced to travel from one segment to another.

The bromeliad plant visually ties the plastic at the upper level and subtly calls attention to the vertical lines.

PLATE 91
Dramatic Involvement

THE BO-TREE AND STUPA

The sacred Bo-Tree of India grows beside the earthy temple wall and is entangled with the serpent, which is on the rim of this container — the stupa. It struggles upward and meets the upper horizontal branch which is the dominant line; it encloses volume.

Visual balance is obtained by the treatment of foliage: One-half of the upright leaf remains solid and is extenuated by the flower; the other half of the leaf has been skeletonized and placed in a horizontal position for counterbalance.

The two lower orange flowers which are enclosed in this volume, satisfy the elements of design. The "V" shaped formation of the petals emphasizes the shape of the branch terminals and foliage.

PLATE 92
The Bo-Tree And Stupa

DOUBLE TALK

The allium stem, when fresh and pliable, was shaped into this circular pattern which cuts through the opening of the vase. In its dried form it has become a permanent part of the composition. A fresh orange flower, round in form, was carefully chosen to complement the inside color of the container, as well as the round openings, and allium blossom.

The vertical line of the container continues upward through the vertical line of the allium stem. This line turns to the left in a circular movement, enclosing the blossom in space.

The decorative vase is distinctive in design which restricts the use of plant materials.

PLATE 93
Double Talk

TALES FROM THE SEA

The dash of waves, created by the plastic lines, surges upward from the parabolic curved container with great force — excitement. Sea gulls sweep downwarc into the waves, investigating the flowers swept ashore by the ocean waves. A barnacled wooden post worn by time and tide is the mooring that counterbalances the arrangement. Coral and sea shells enhance the story of the sea.

This is an excellent example of opposing forces. The dynamic motion in the waves and in the flight of birds is opposed by the static, vertical line of the post. This opposition is illusive — reminiscent of wird, sea, and sand.

The principle of unity is satisfied by the association of materials.

PLATE 94
Tales From The Sea

PLATE 95
Kona Surf

KONA SURF

Hawaiian black volcanic rock of shore line inspired this rhythmic arrangement. The circular lines of the container dictate the lines of this piece. These lines continue through the waves of black aspidistra leaves, blending with the plastic curved filaments of sea foam. They engulf the stylized lotus blossom — natural in form but man-made. Lily petals have been reversed to form the corolla around the pin-cusion protea (P. lutens) which is the stamen.

This is a decorative arrangement which complements a black and white decor. Modern interiors require dramatic floral designs to blend with their settings.

PARABOLIC ENERGY

Dynamic force, established by the power of the parabolic container, is extended by the lines of the cycas fronds. This upward line breaks into the atmosphere and extends into infinity, dissipating its force. The lower line of the cycas branch continues the circular motion of the container, defining volume, which confines the beautiful tropical blossom. This flower creates the calm atmosphere in the turbulent forces created by all the lines. It acts as the directrix to the parabola. There is also an inner counter-clockwise, dynamic force established by the tip of the broad leaf of this blossom. This energy confines the circular motion to this central volume.

PLATE 96
Parabolic Ene

PLATE 97
Oppositional Forces

OPPOSITIONAL FORCES

In the arranging of flowers, it is the general tendency to follow the lines of the natural growth of plants; that is, placing flowers to correspond with foliage.

The linear foliage establishes this crescent design. However, the three anthurium blossoms are placed in direct opposition to this concept but complete the lower portion of the cresent. They add dramatic emphasis and distinction. The colors of red and green are in contrast. Even though there is tension in oppositional forces, there is unity and rhythmic harmony.

ATE 98
omeward Flight

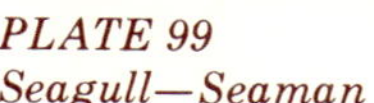

PLATE 99
Seagull—Seaman

PLATE 100
Seagull At Sunset

HOMEWARD FLIGHT

The welded sculpture, "Sea Gulls", by Reg Coghlan, an abstraction, suggests flight at sunset. They are preceded by white, ceramic gulls near the shore; the metal ones appear to be in shadow. This piece is suspended from an iron rod secured to a cross-section of a walnut tree. A white, ceramic, parabolic curved container holds the arrangement. Cycas foliage, feathered to represent wings, stylized, and painted a brilliant pink-orange, depicts the evening glow of sunset. Pin-cushion protea blossoms, in brilliant orange, with abstract corollas of lily petals, form the floral accent. Each petal is a repetitious form of white sea gull wing tips. Drama is enacted with vibrant display of color and shapes. Great depth is created by the illusion of positive and negative forces in colors and forms.

Pure abstract is form created for its own purpose; it has its own set of values, creating beauty. The sculptor and painter use their media, which covers a wide scope of materials, but the floral arranger is restricted to plant materials and accessories. Flower or plant material may be changed to satisfy the composition. Distortion may be used to express abstraction, but this quality becomes trite unless it has definite meaning and purpose. Distortion was necessary to meet the demands of this unique design.

PLATE 101
Homeward Flight—Detail

RHYTHM IN STEEL

The rhythmic lines, created by the steel shavings, carve their own design in space. Their coarse texture is tempered by their graceful, curvilinear movement which is in contrast to the finely textured camellia.

The clear glass plate is compatible in form and texture. A feeling of suspension is in evidence.

The base is Victorian which is reminiscent of past earthly experiences. Its decorative curves are repeated in the blossoms and steel shavings. The rhythm flows gently from base to top.

PLATE 102
Rhythm In Steel

MUSICAL NOTES

This design shows the influence of Piet Mondrian (1872-1944), whose compositions of impeccable order reduced the image to non-representational forms of line and color. He stated that paintings must be freed from their bondage of imitation of nature and allowed to exist for themselves. He theorized that painting was on a flat surface and therefore, must be allowed to declare itself and not be falsified by the imitation of volume and perspective.

The right angle elbow of the container, a stylized pitcher, and the right angles of the bleached wisteria vines enclose space and create patterns. The horizontal lines of the platform of the container and the stone base are repeated in the horizontal lines of the wisteria. These horizontal lines are representative of the bars (staff) on which the musical notes of the ball-shaped flowers appear. They create a burst of color, and their shapes are repeated in the simulated negative notes of the circles of wisteria, thus creating "eye sound". This sound soars upward through the central axis, which acts as a stabilizing balance.

PLATE 103
Musical Notes

PLATE 104
The Viking

THE VIKING

This curved, parabolic, ceramic piece of blue and green was patterned from an antique Chinese stirrup. Its form suggests a Viking ship.

A blossom of banksia with its "rick-rack" shaped leaves completes the form of the container, adding force to the forward motion.

The exotic anthuriums are enclosed in the volume, but add directional force. The blossoms are reminicent of the flowers found by the men who sailed "Kon-Tiki"; the bamboo suggests the raft on which they sailed.

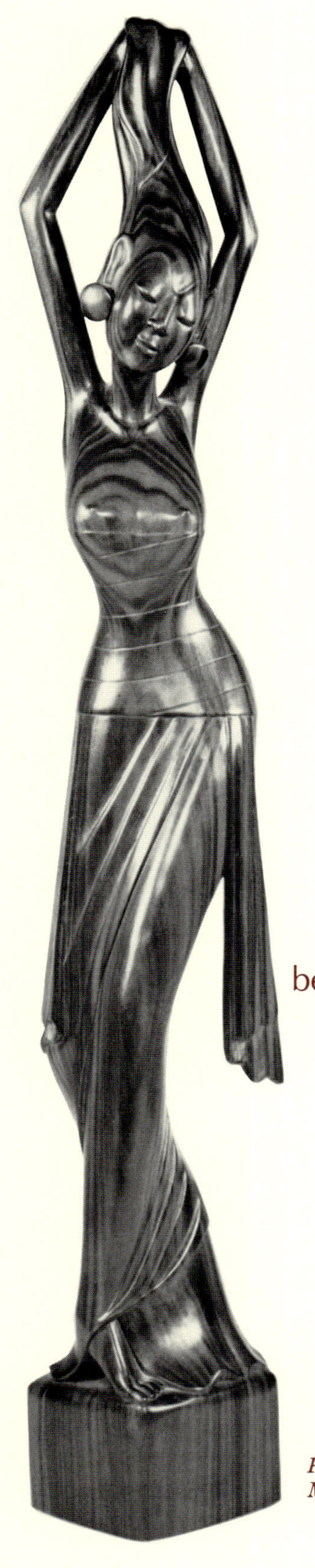

PLATE 105
Mystic Pose

POISED SERPENT

The striking wooden serpent of rough, masculine lines is poised on the edge of the container. It strikes at the ghostly black birds-of-paradise (Strelitzia Nicolai), prehistoric in form, causing them to burst into confused flight. Red flame ginger pulsates at the heart of the design, adding life to the somber dark forms. Patterns are etched into interesting shapes which direct the eye in many directions.

MYSTIC POSE

Mystic Pose, a striking figurine of grace and beauty, speaks of the vibrant life of Indonesia. The red ginger and her pose are complementary.

PLATE 106
Poised Serpe

Principle of Texture____

—is relative, associational in value. It is valued only by comparison. The wooden figure and the clam shell have textured kinship that is compatible to the coral and bamboo raft. The convolutions of the shell are repeated by the petals of the red amaryllis. The upward lines of the foliage reinforce the dynamic motion of the head. (Plate 108).

PLATE 107
Sea Horse

Plastic form (Plate 107), which by coincidence took the profile of a sea horse, is similar in form to the wooden horse. The natural inherent trait of the mind is to associate objects of familiar form. These pieces are abstractions as illustrated by the author.

PEGASUS

The powerful abstract image of a horse is strongly conveyed to the viewer. The rough, scaly, texture of this wooden figure was sculptured by years of submersion in the placid waters of a lake bed. Whereas, a smooth patina would be the result of tidal action of the sea.

PLATE 1(
Pegasus

Principle of Balance___

Balance and proportion are interdependent; they are inseparable. Balance is equilibrium—the division of measured weights or quantities to either side of an imaginary central axis, a center of gravity.

Balance is achieved when the elements of a design are so composed that they give a feeling of stability. However, in balance the weights may be equal but the comparative sizes of the materials may be out of proportion in their relationship lacking visual balance. The units are not scaled to be harmonious to each other or to their placement in a given area.

Principle of Proportion___

(Scale) — compares the relationship of the units of composition to each other in size and quantity, and are scaled to their setting or placement. Form logically follows function. Non-objective form needs no function; therefore, form is its only need for being. It exists for itself only.

study—
FALLEN MAN"—Tom Barringer

MOTHER EARTH

This spectacular piece of wood dominates its surrounding. It is beautifully eroded, telling its own story. We appreciate its form — the grain — its lines — we appreciate the knot-hole, knowing that a limb was served. It had leaves that nourished the tree, gave color in spring, summer, and fall, and that it was a resting place for bird and beast. Its varied forms remind us of the struggle with nature to survive. The center formation of vertical lines, terminating in a mushroom cap, relates to the similarly shaped cloud of smoke from an atomic explosion. The outer rims surrounding this formation suggest the womb of Mother Earth. We marvel at its beauty to which we relate an experience of our association with nature and science.

When man searches for scientific knowledge through the years, to enable him to understand nature's secrets, they are revealed to him. Here we have a story unfolded in a natural work of art. Birds-of-paradise add a colorful note of life which spring from volcanic rock at its base. The primitive Nubian carved head tells its own story of precivilized man who soon will harness the powers of earth.

Bold statements are made clear in each element of this design. Birds (Strelitzia) sparkle, eroded wood expresses timelessness, and the figurine is a symbol of the dawn of man.

PLATE 109
Mother Earth

PLATE 110
Balinese Gate

There is a unique, distinctive type of architecture which exists on the island of Bali. The entrances (Plates 110 & 111) to their temples are far different in design than any other culture on earth. The builders of these ornate structures constructed the entrances in two half-units with steps in the center which lead to the temple. Note—there is no arch connecting the units. Grotesquely carved stone gods are placed on either side of the steps to deter evil spirits.

PLATE 111
Balinese Gate — Detail

PLATE 112
Balinese Temple

BALINESE TEMPLE

This peculiar treatment of temple gates conjure up much mysticism that influences floral design. This is a tall, azure blue container with hieroglyphics written in horizontal lines which depict the carvings of the temple walls. A tree has been split in half and placed on either side of the container to depict the architectural motif, simulating the gates. A column of yellow line flowers are massed between the two half-trees representing a pagoda. Two brilliant red dessert spoons poise at the entrance, as devil dancers, ready to perform their religious rites.

PLATE 113
Temple Of The Dawn

CYCAS TOWER

The male cone of the cycas (C. revoluta), sago palm, is like a towering exclamation point which dominates the horizon. The cycas cone corresponds perfectly to the accompanying picture of the Temple of the Dawn (Bangkok), each a tower of strength and beauty. The cone is accented by the abstract cycas leaf in pagoda silhouette. Stylized palm frond hands rise from the camellias, in sheltering fashion, and continue the line of the cymbidium orchids. Their ruby lips add color and interest to plant materials.

Man — the designer — is greatly inspired by forms of nature.

PLATE 114
Cycas Towe

PLATE 115
Primitive Cross

PRIMITIVE CROSS

The container, a ceramic piece, is reminiscent of the silhouette of an ancient king with head-dress, indicated by the square flange. The container holds a stylized cross of trimmed cycas foliage which recalls the rice thatched pagodas. The floral sequence is a characteristic design of primitive people. The urge to design, to create pattern, is innate in all races of people as exemplified in Plates 32, 33. Geometric symbols are seen on all continents, and mythological connotation is attached to these symbols to give meaning.

The ritual platform base is compatible with the design.

PLATE 116
Rice Thatched Pago

PLATE 117
Three Cylinders

PLATE 118
Three Cylinders I

PLATE 119
Three Cylinders III

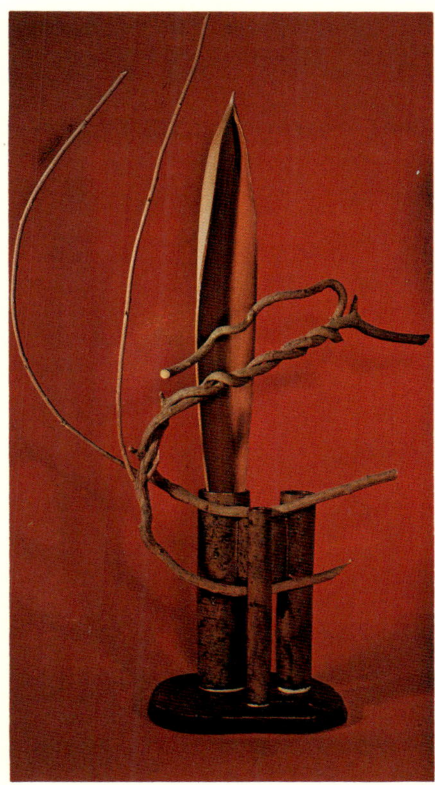

THREE CYLINDERS I

Three cylinders of various diameters invite the designer to explore new possibilities for self-expression. The severe palm spathe, compatible in color and earthy qualities, makes a firm statement demanding attention. A vine-branch involves the container with the palm spathe, creating open areas that express motion — activity.

THREE CYLINDERS II

A pyramidal column of white gladioli rises to its full height from a mass of orange roses which repeats the triangle. Their conical shapes complement the silhouette of the palm spathe. Note the three lines terminate at the apex which are opposing the three horizontal stems of the vines.

THREE CYLINDERS III

In this design the palm spathe and flowers have been removed. An entirely different design has been created by adding allium blossoms (A. giganteum). Their round form accentuates the parabolic curves of the vine, giving it greater importance.

Principle of Color

preference is due to two factors: First, a person's nervous reaction; secondly, the influence of environment (education) of a person. The intensity of the sun affects color preference. In southern climes, due to the brilliancy of the sun, nature has given the birds and flowers brilliant hues, and the people a liking for strong spices and colors. Moving northward, the less intense the sun's rays, the preference is for muted colors. In the extreme north, black and white predominate.

All colors are beautiful: It is the use of a color, its intensity, its combination with other colors, and the personal reaction to color, that makes it pleasing or objectionable. There is no criteria by which to judge color combinations.

No single system has been devised that successfully organizes the study of color phenomena. How hues relate to each other, and how persons react to them, and various combinations, is still in question. Therefore, each person may determine his own reaction and theory on the basis of his education and experience.

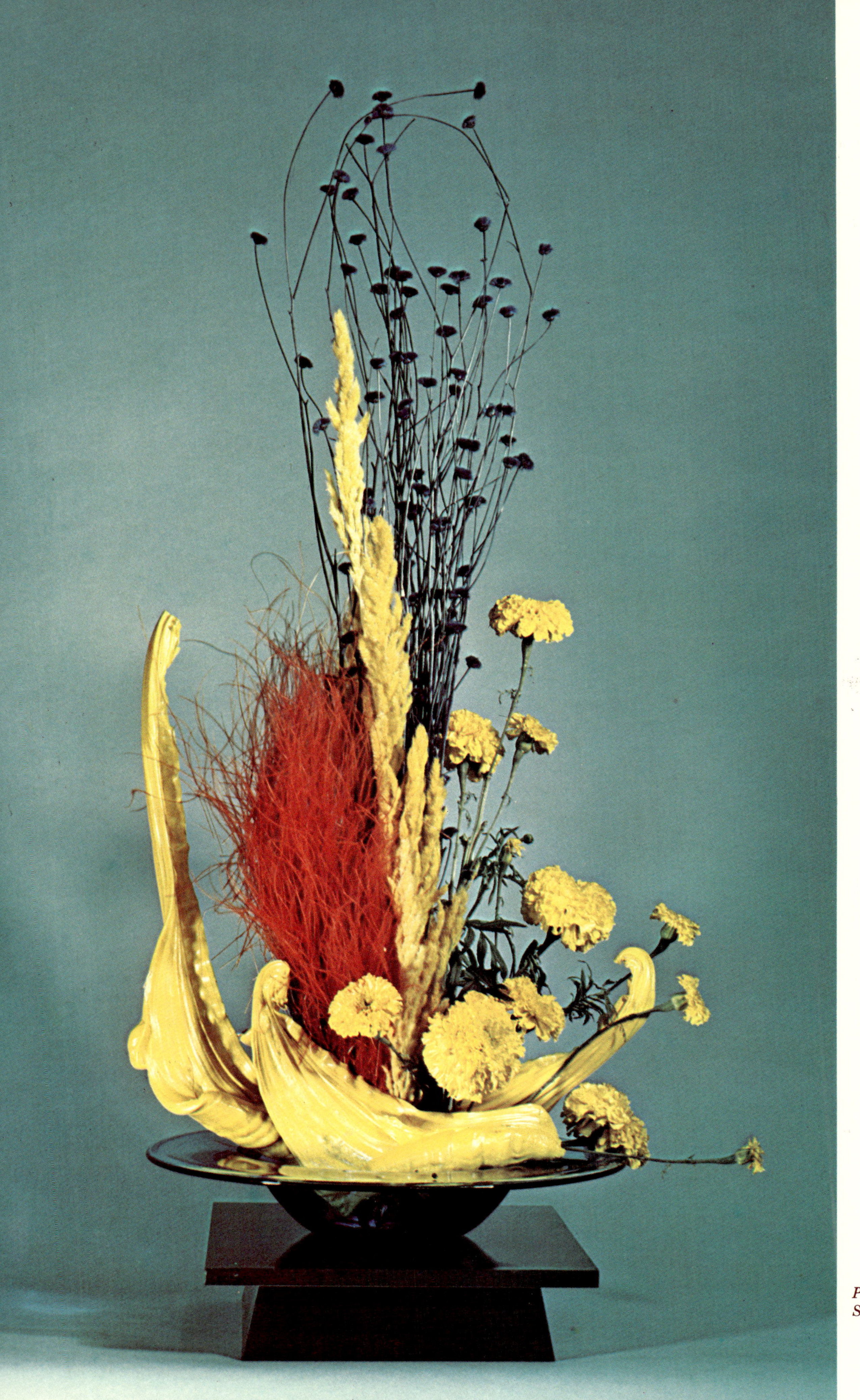

PLATE 120
Study In Color

STUDY IN COLORS

The three basic primary colors — red, yellow, and blue — show their characteristic properties and dimensions in this illustration.

RED appears to advance; therefore, the less in quantity will counterbalance large amounts of yellow.

YELLOW is bright, cheerful, and increases in appearance. The yellow plastic and marigolds dominate the design.

BLUE is receding, creating the feeling of depth. The large, blue bowl and blue background give stability to its counterparts.

KAVA BOWL

The brilliant colors of the Fiji Islands are portrayed in this design. Florets of red, green, and purple are massed for weight and color. There is an interplay of motion and color, causing the eye to travel over the design with pleasure. The tri-dimensional color values reflect an awareness of equilibrium, but the design is not static. The eyes move backward and forward from one area to another, due partly to lack of a center point of interest. A single focal point would draw attention. Rhythm and movement are keenly felt. Had the red area been alternated by the other color areas, this rhythm would have been halted. Note the movement of red tints upward in the design. Should yellow or another vibrant color replace the green or purple area, competition would result. Color perception is evident.

Ti foliage moves inward and outward, giving direction to this rhythm. There is a curved line suggested by the cowrie shell and directed by the ti foliage through the red flowers, and on upward into the canna foliage. The curvilinear line is reinforced by the group of lilies (Lilium regale). They speak of the influence of the missionaries. Garlands of similar flowers are used by the warriors around the body as part of the kava ceremonial dances.

PLATE 121
Kava Bowl

TURQUOISE AND CORAL

Indian jewelry — the throne of the mighty warrior and many other romantic ideas are conjured in this inspiring design. The mind runs rampant. Colors vibrate with loud cymbal clashes, moving forward and backward. Color dominates the picture. Each participant of form and color in the design clearly makes a statement. It is unusual to see the receding quality of blue, smaller in quantity, yet equal the greater quantity of red — the advancing color. The container, of earthy tones, has broad planes and defined lines of horizontal stratification which are repeated in the staccato placement of flowers. The strong, stately position of the amaryllis equalizes the strength of the container, and visually balances the heavy heliconia bracts. Although definite horizontal lines dominate even to the cut ends of the foliage, there is a strong vertical tension stressed in opposition by the stems. The triangle is sketched by the turquoise desert spoons, and is clearly restated in the cardone puffs. The heliconia (H. Caribaea var. purpurea) form the outer pyramid which embraces the whole composition.

There is sheer beauty and sensual pleasure of juxtaposition of shapes and colors. The eye is induced to move up these horizontal planes, step by step, to the apex. Color contrast emphasizes this stratified value.

PLATE 122
Turquoise And Cora

PLATE 123
Pagan Rites 1

PAGAN RITES I

Hands of heliconia reach upward and unite in pagan worship. The stems of the leaves are cut horizontally to work in opposition to the strong vertical lines. Thus, emphasis is placed at the apex — the point at which the hands join. A rectangular volume is enclosed wherein the limited action takes place. Three priestesses are poised in respectful silence. The clean cut lines rise from the container, leaving it free to make its own statement. It is dramatic! There is a static beauty that holds one in reverence as though the pagan altar is prepared for the sacrificial rites.

PAGAN RITES II

Turquoise plastic delineates the square space of flower stems, which dominates the composition with its strong color, but subdues the importance of the container. Rectangles compete with rectangles. The turquoise line entwines itself into position with a firm grasp, and divides the entire composition into two rectangles. Rectangles are formed one above the other, which are visually equal in size.

One cannot penetrate the pictorial space — he is forbidden by the turquoise barrier. One is excited, but is prevented from walking into the two dimensional space.

The square and rectangular patterns in floral design present a problem because of the equalization of the geometrical right angles. Distinction is achieved by color, selection, and placement of materials. (See Plate 81.)

PLATE 124
Pagan Rites II

PLATE 125
Chinese Blue

CHINESE BLUE

There is visual balance in this composition that pleases. The Chinese antique vase is dominant. The proteas (Protea neriifolia) reflect bold character which hold interest in their exotic form and color. They do not compete, but enhance the beauty of the container.

Weeping willow branches frame the objects, and carefully delineate the design. The top branch has been bent forward, purposely, to abruptly stop the eye from traveling upward. The lower branch curves gracefully in its purpose to return the eye upward into the design. Thus, the branches enclose the picture plane.

KING AND QUEEN

The kava bowl signifies that a ceremony is to be held in honor of a king and queen, each represented by a king protea blossom (P. cynaroides). The large flower in forward position is representative of the king, the smaller one the queen. The cowrie shell, valued as money, points to the guest of honor. Dances will be held as represented by the motion of the black leaves. Papyrus (Cyperus papyrus) tassels are indigenous to this area. The tablecloth is of tapa which is made from the bark of the mulberry tree; it is painted in abstract design.

These twin arrangements are united by line and similar plant materials. The circular motion of the bowl swirls into lines of black foliage which enclose spherical volume. Great depth is created by the swirling action of foliage which terminates at its apex.

PLATE 126
King And Queen

STAR WARS

Star
Wars

pulsars

GALAXIES

quasars

the universe

suspension!

SPACE!

Dynamic balance—ecology!

All forces of nature and the universe are working in co-ordination—seemingly from all directions—YET controlled.

This rare ceramic form of directional angles, expressive of our time, forces the mind's eye to travel to the great beyond. Brilliant, clear cut, precise anthurium blossoms confines the forces, defining volume, creating an entity within itself. The viewer's eye is forced to search for boundaries.

Anthurium, whose form, color and smooth plastic-like surface, are the only floral material which satisfy the design set by the "container." The eye movement from voids to solids creates the shooting stars and flying objects from outer space. This design recalls the great art that Alexander Calder created in his fantastic mobiles introducing a new art form—releasing any attachment to earth, Space unlimited.

LATE 127
tar Wars

SADDLE BAG

How the west was won. Water! Water!—that element so needed to sustain life is expressed in this abstraction.

An ordinary pre-civil war leather saddle bag inspired this ceramic artist to tell an old story in art form, that has made history—an abstraction that holds memories untold.

Water, expressed by the variegated aspididtra, spills forth, flowing and gurgling from the spout thus giving life and movement to the arrangement. The bromeliad, Vriesca Duvalis Rex, is the flower representing life necessary to continue the journey of the lone traveler. One stands in awe of the mystic it holds to the viewer's attention.

PLATE 12
Saddle Ba

PLATE 129
Garden Sculpture

MOBILE—STABILE—THE TREE

Kinetic art — activity is in the sensitive mobile suspended from the spectacular stabile of palm spathes. This design is eight feet in height. The palm sheaths (Coco Arecastum Romanziffiaum var. australe) are glued together at the center and are bound with coconut fiber rope for security. This rope adds texture and interest to the design. Holes were drilled into the stabile which hold iron rods. Earthy and natural materials in their preserved form which are suspended in sensitive balance, move gently with the breeze. Fresh flowers may be added in the area formed by the palm sheaths at top center, or in the parabolic flanges that float in the air.

Balance means stability — equilibrium. Proper placement of main stems establishes the kind of balance, whether symmetrical or asymmetrical. There must be an equalizing force to either side of a central axis to maintain this sense of balance.

In this design there is perfect balance achieved, but not perfect symmetry.

PLATE 130
Mobile—Stabile
The Tree

"THE WAY of the EAGLE"
A fleeting moment of action - dynamic force expressed in perfect harmony.

The essence of ecology is captured in this magnificent bronze sculpture. This unique piece, portraying survival of the fittest in wild life, requires artful handling of floral materials.

The flowers (Curcuma Roscoeana and pine cone ginger, Zingiber zerumbet) were chosen for their distinctive shapes and color variation.

A piece of water-worn cypress was selected to emphasize the rhythmic curves of the wings. Its weight ties this flight in space to earth, enhancing the powerful attitude of the entire composition.

PLATE 131
The Way Of The Eagle

If I have inspired
a thought
an idea
a form
a dream

If I have opened the window of my soul
through this medium of flowers

And we have viewed the beauty
of God
of Nature
of Universal order

Then life has been a prayer.

M. 'Buddy' Benz

UNNUMBERED ILLUSTRATIONS

AF583397
Koala

how to make a

Koala

Choose your paper.
Grab the pre-made sheet or colour
one in yourself.

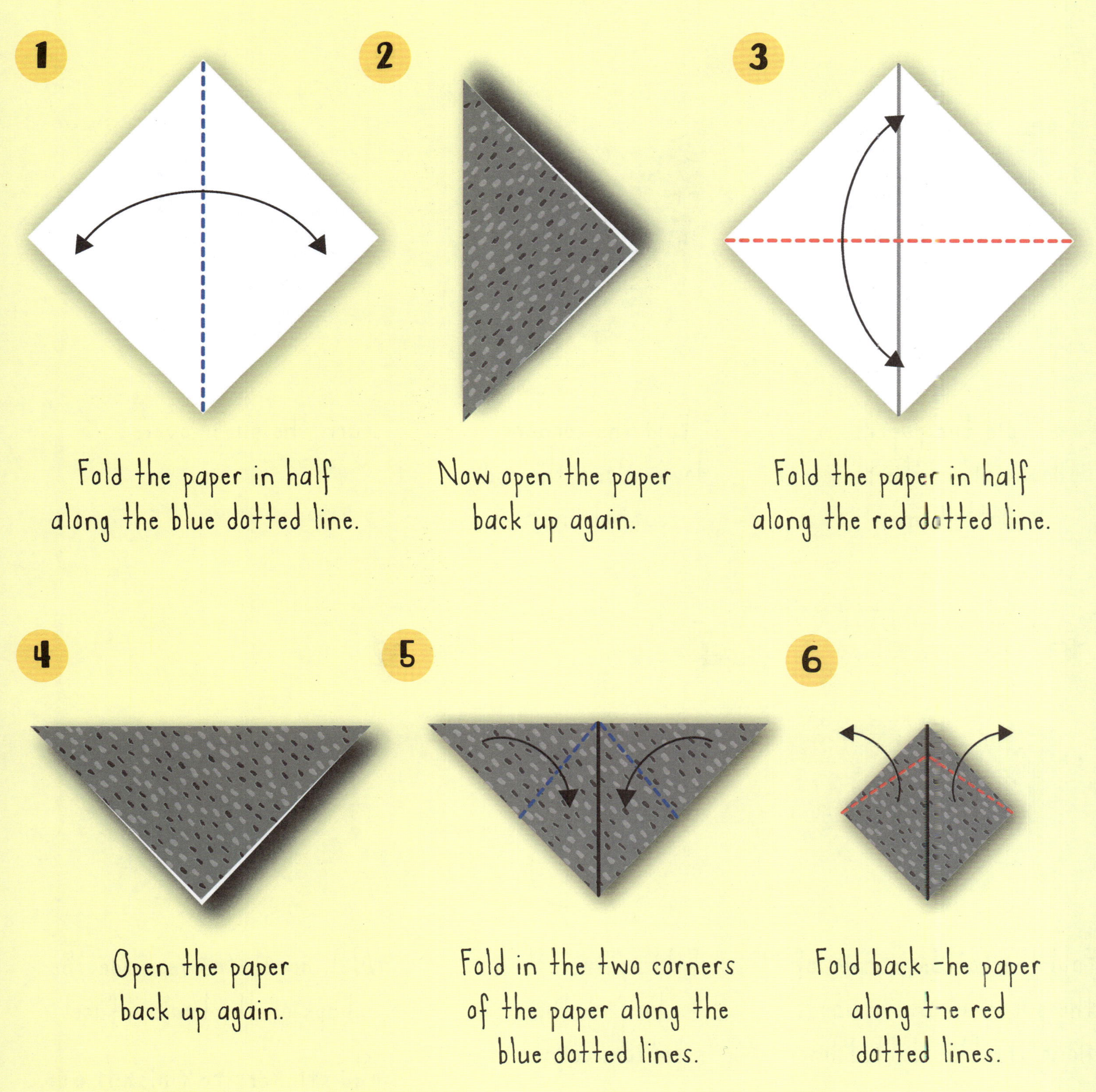
1
Fold the paper in half along the blue dotted line.
2
Now open the paper back up again.
3
Fold the paper in half along the red dotted line.
4
Open the paper back up again.
5
Fold in the two corners of the paper along the blue dotted lines.
6
Fold back the paper along the red dotted lines.

7

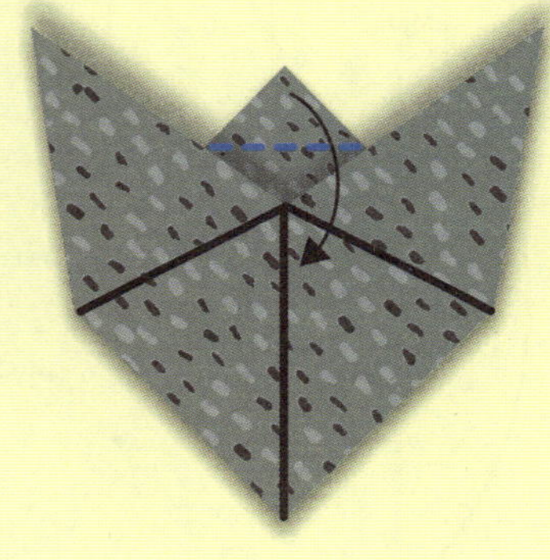

Fold the paper down along the blue dotted line.

8

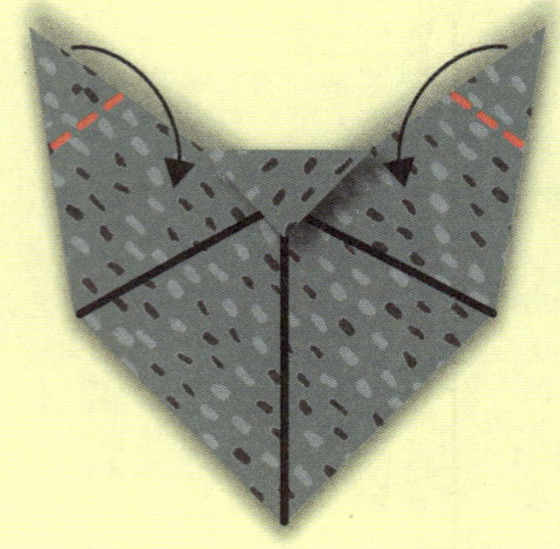

Fold the corners down along the red dotted lines.

9

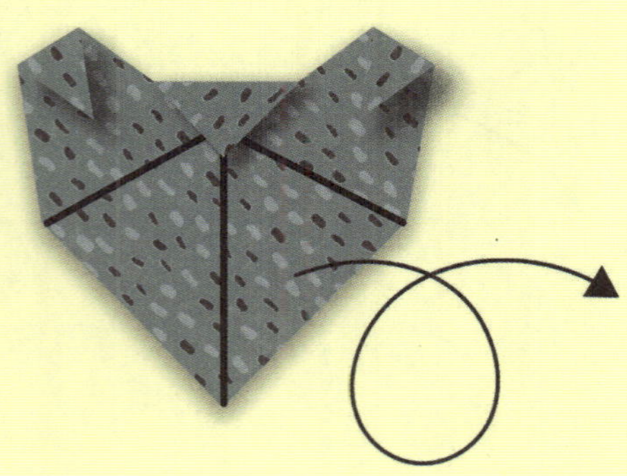

Turn the paper over.

10

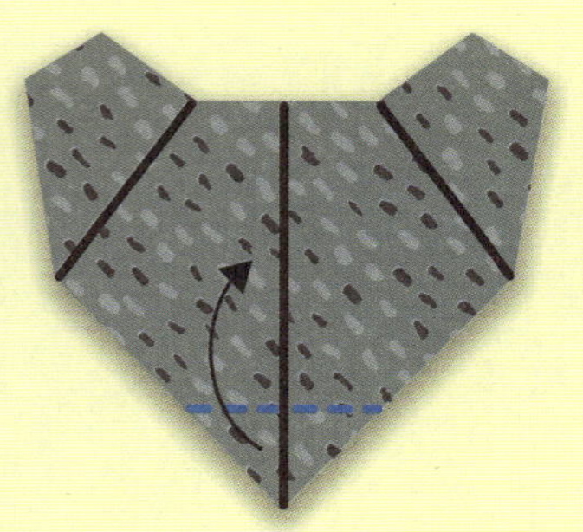

Fold the bottom corner of the paper up and inwards along the blue dotted line.

11

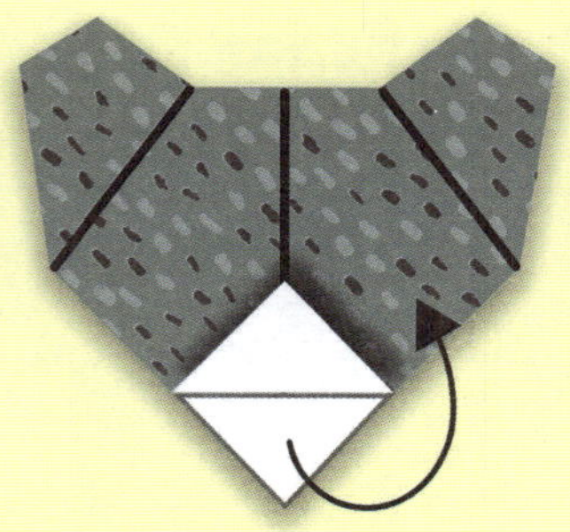

Fold up the other half of the bottom corner.

12

Well done! You've made the shape of the koala's face!

Add stickers to finish it off.

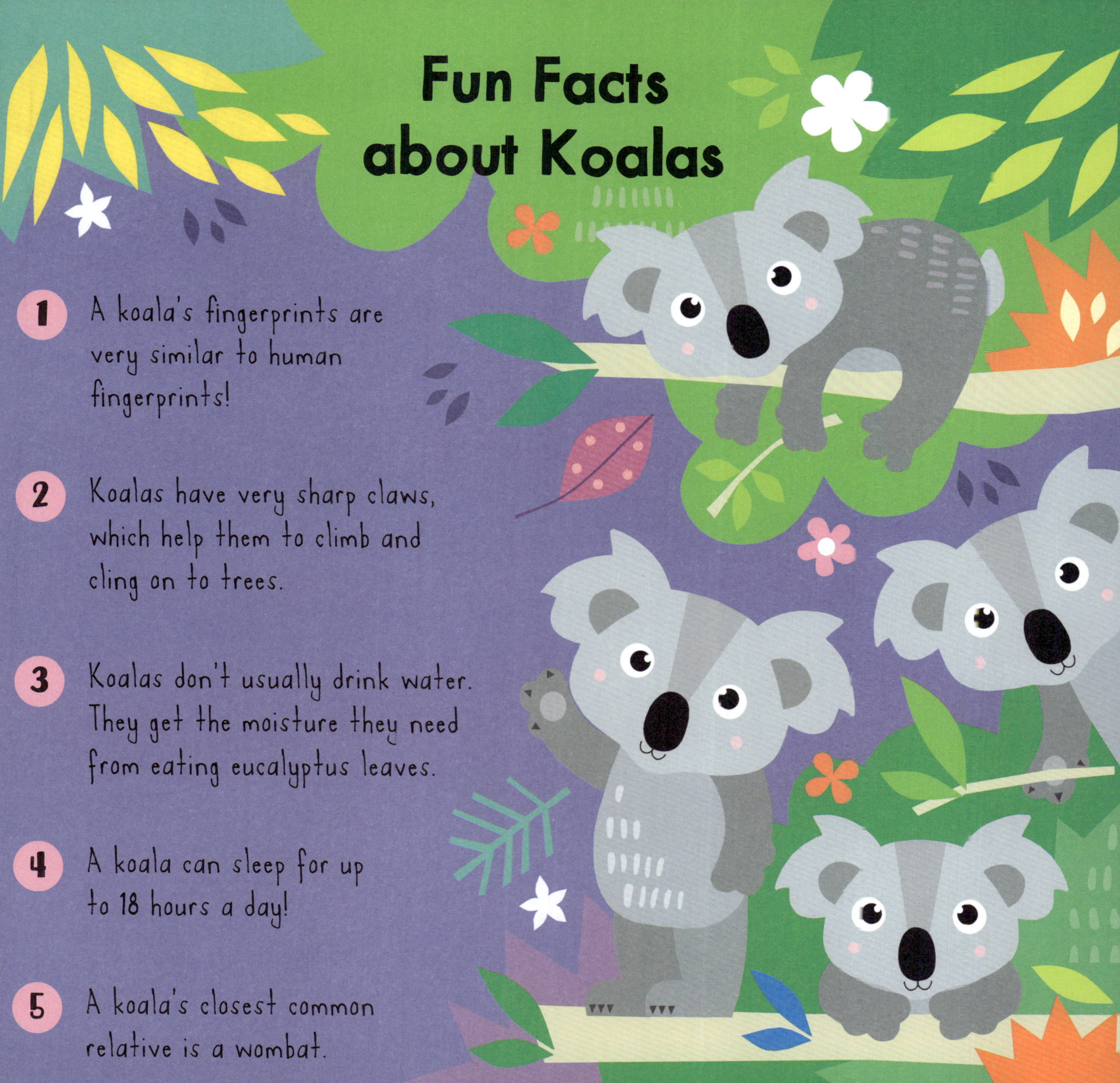

Fun Facts about Koalas

1. A koala's fingerprints are very similar to human fingerprints!

2. Koalas have very sharp claws, which help them to climb and cling on to trees.

3. Koalas don't usually drink water. They get the moisture they need from eating eucalyptus leaves.

4. A koala can sleep for up to 18 hours a day!

5. A koala's closest common relative is a wombat.

Find and Count

Koala | Green leaf | Purple leaf | Flower

Koala - 7 | Green leaf - 8 | Purple leaf - 5 | Flower - 8

Tiger

how to make a
Tiger
Choose your paper.
Grab the pre-made sheet or colour
one in yourself.

1

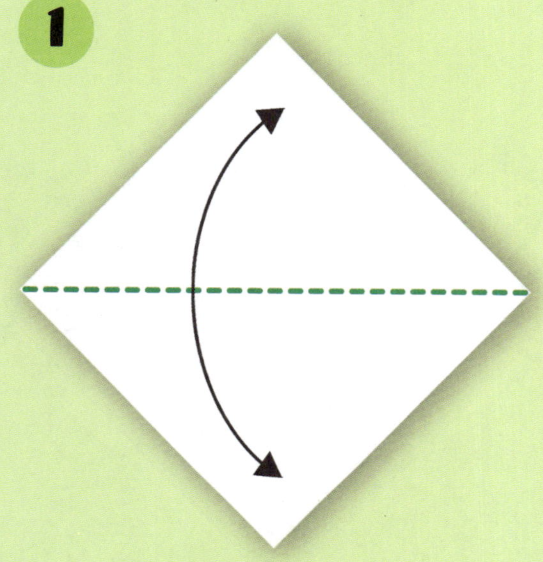

Fold the paper in half along the green dotted line.

2

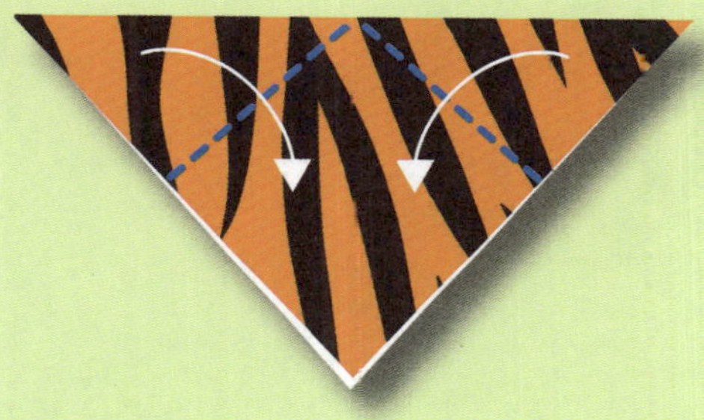

Fold in the two corners of the paper along the b lue dotted lines.

3

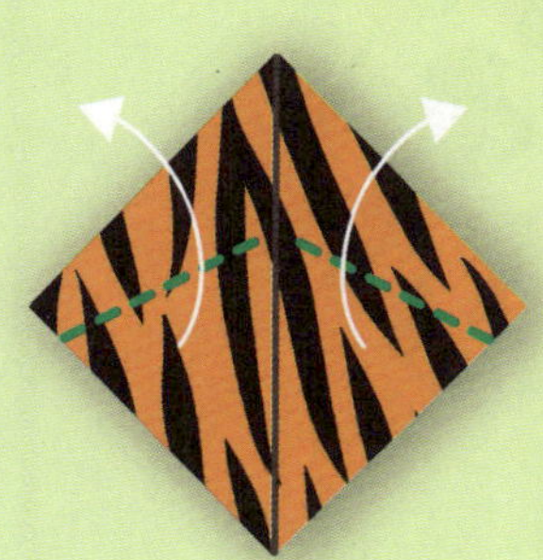

Open the paper out along the green dotted lines.

4

Fold in the two small tabs on each side.

5

Fold the paper down along the blue dotted line.

6

Turn the paper over.

Fold the bottom corner of the paper up and in along the green dotted line.

Fold up the other half of the bottom corner.

9

Fold down the tip of the fold you made in step 9.

10

Well done! You've made the shape of the tiger's face!

Add stickers to finish it off.

Terrific Tiger Facts

1 Tigers are the largest wild cats in the world!

2 A tiger can run up to 65 kilometres per hour!

3 It is believed that tigers have been around for almost 2 million years!

4 No two tigers have the same stripes, each is unique - much like human fingerprints.

5 Tigers love the water. They often swim and bathe in lakes.

Trace and Colour

Can you draw the other half of the tiger's face?

Panda

how to make a
Panda
Choose your paper.
Grab the pre-made sheet or colour
one in yourself.

1. Fold the paper in half along the blue dotted line.

2. Open the paper up again.

3. Fold the paper in half along the red dotted line.

4. Open out the paper.

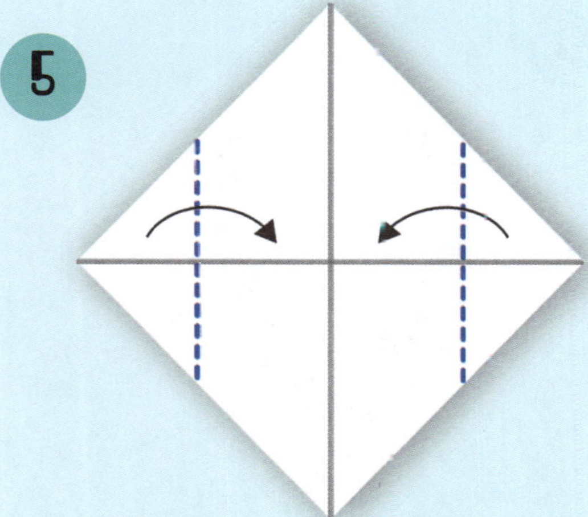

5. Fold in the two sides of the paper along the blue dotted lines.

6

Fold the top tip of the paper down backwards along the blue dotted line.

7

Turn the paper over.

8

Fold the paper down along the red dotted line.

Fold the bottom corner of the paper up and in along the blue dotted line.

Well done! You've made the shape of the panda's face!

Add stickers to finish it off.

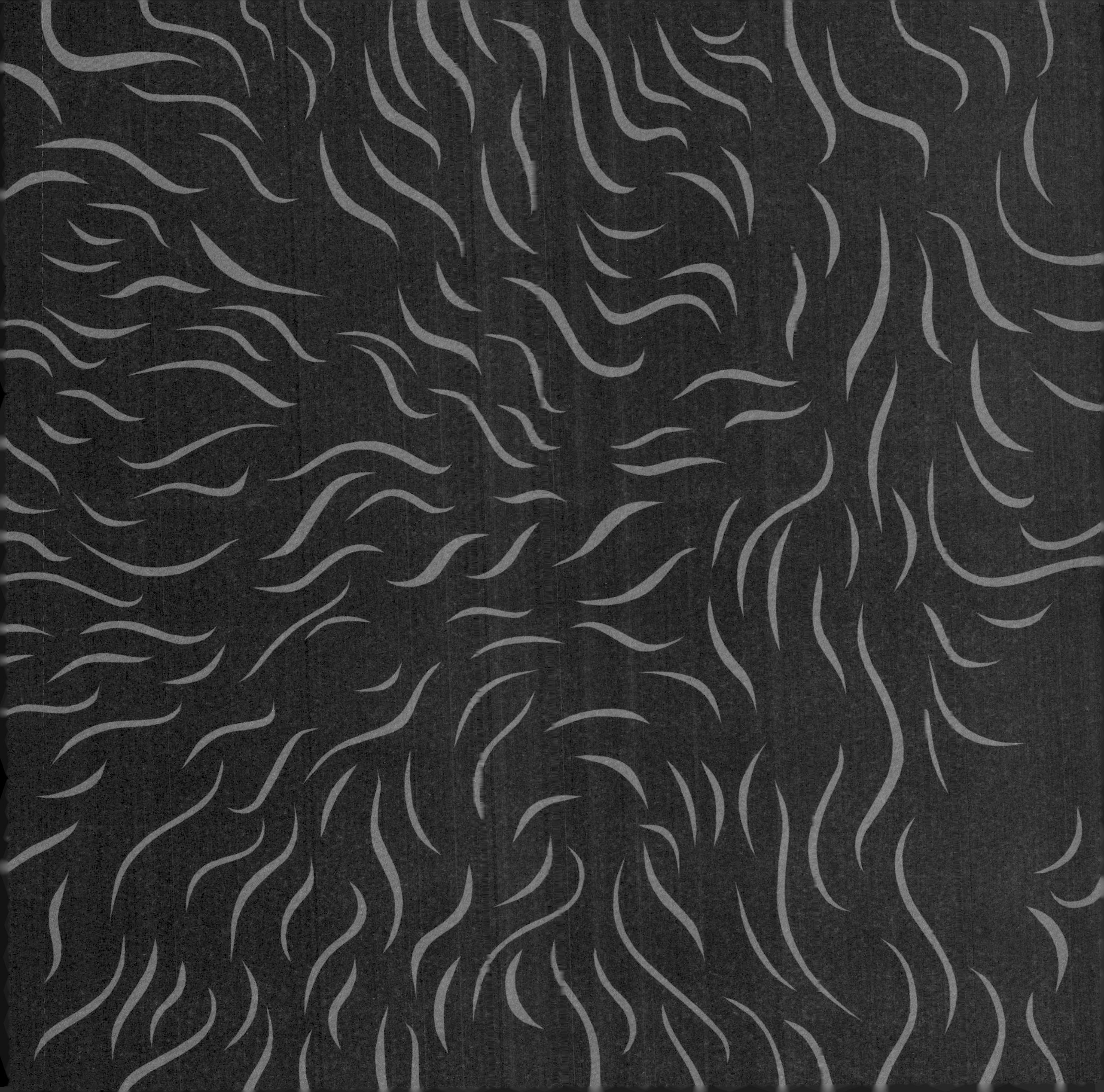

Pawsome Pandas Facts

1. Bamboo makes up 99 per cent of a panda's diet!

2. Pandas don't hibernate. Instead, when winter comes around they head lower down the mountains to warmer temperatures.

3. Pandas are born blind. They don't open their eyes until around six to eight weeks after they're born.

4. When baby pandas are born they're about as long as a pencil!

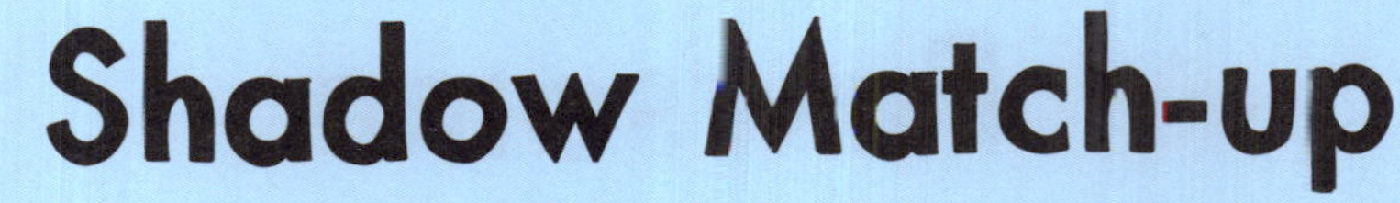

Shadow Match-up

Can you find the panda's matching shadow?

Elephant

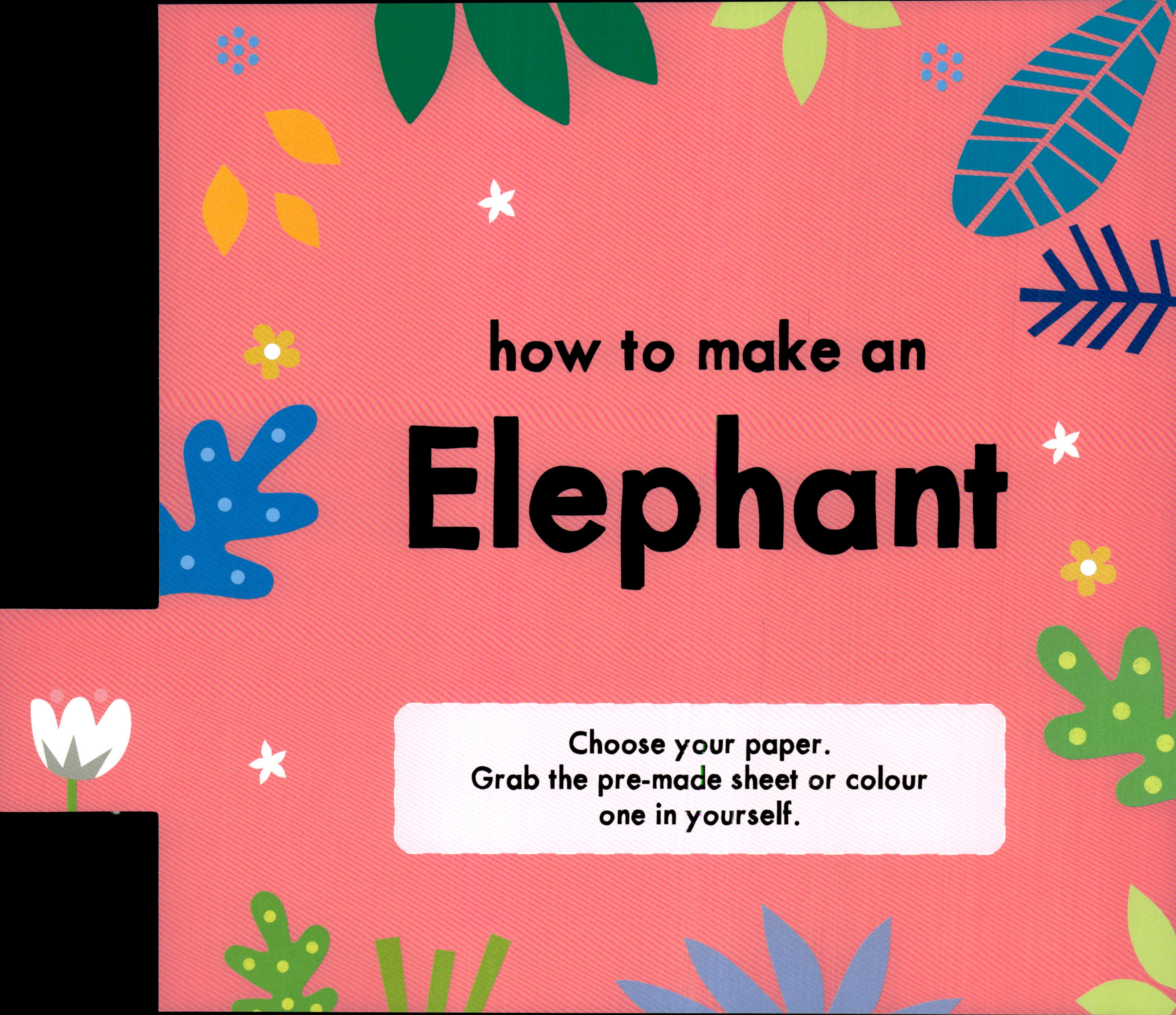
how to make an
Elephant
Choose your paper.
Grab the pre-made sheet or colour
one in yourself.

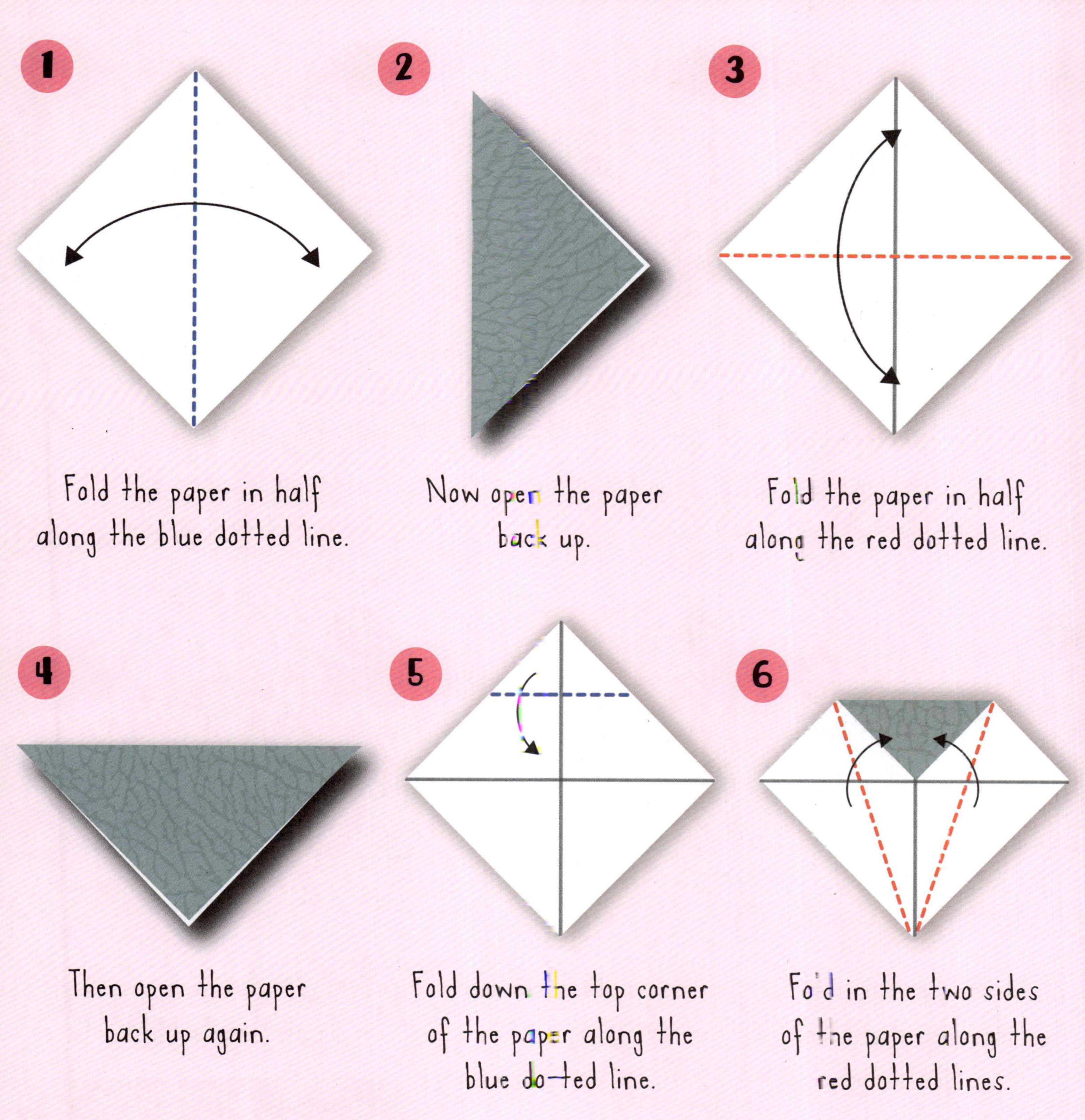
1
Fold the paper in half along the blue dotted line.
2
Now open the paper back up.
3
Fold the paper in half along the red dotted line.
4
Then open the paper back up again.
5
Fold down the top corner of the paper along the blue dotted line.
6
Fold in the two sides of the paper along the red dotted lines.

7

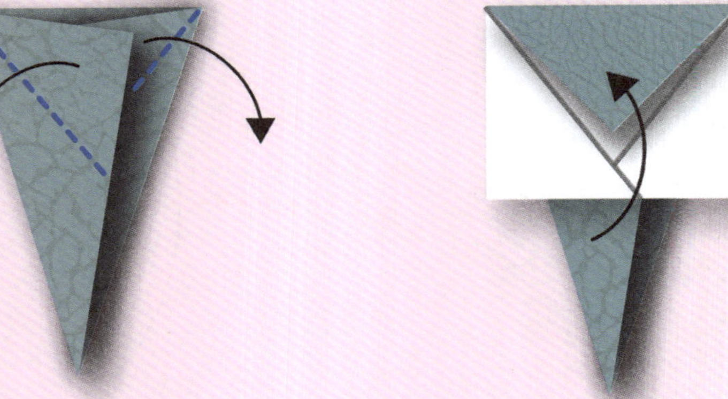

Fold the two top corners of the folds down along the blue dotted lines.

8

Fold the bottom piece up and over.

9

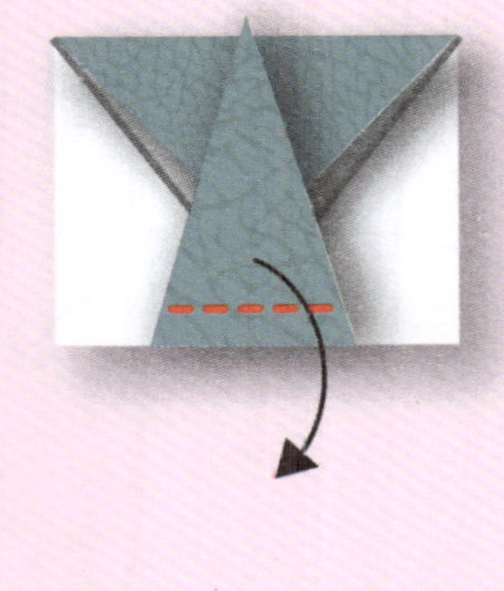

Fold the paper back over along the red dotted line.

10

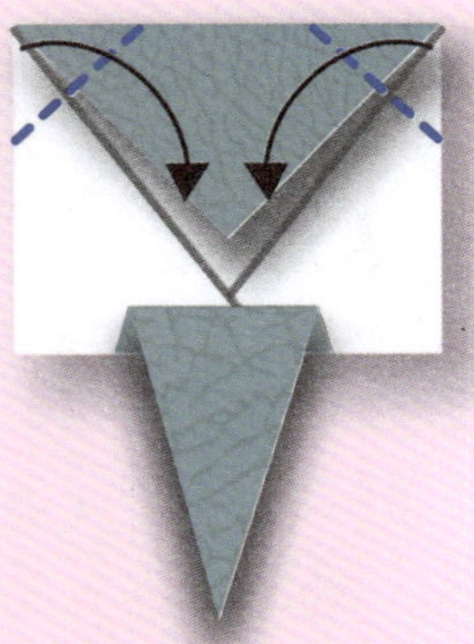

Fold the two top corner edges in along the blue dotted lines.

11

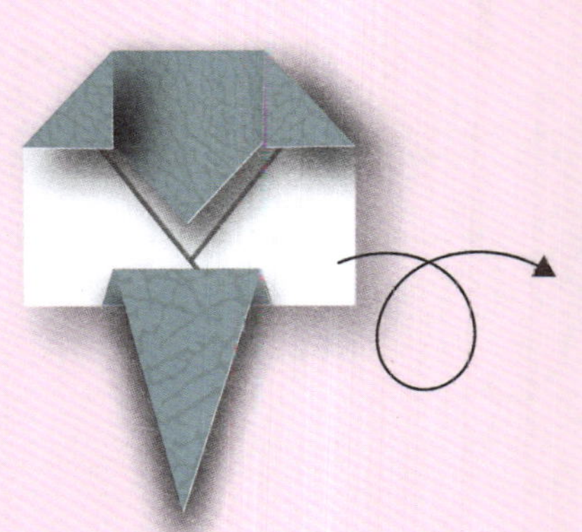

Turn the paper over.

12

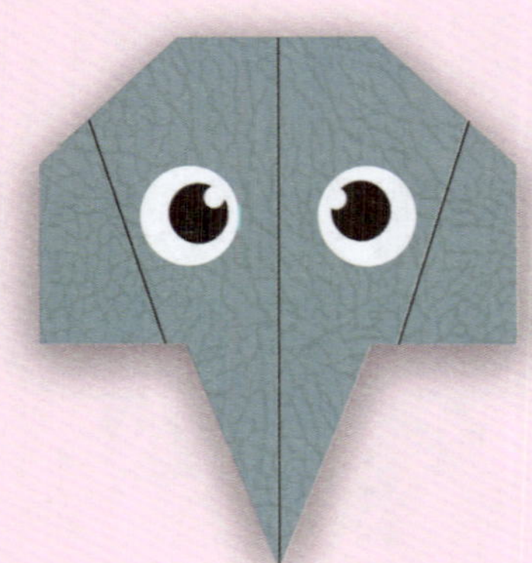

Well done! You've made the shape of the elephant's face!

Add stickers to finish it off.

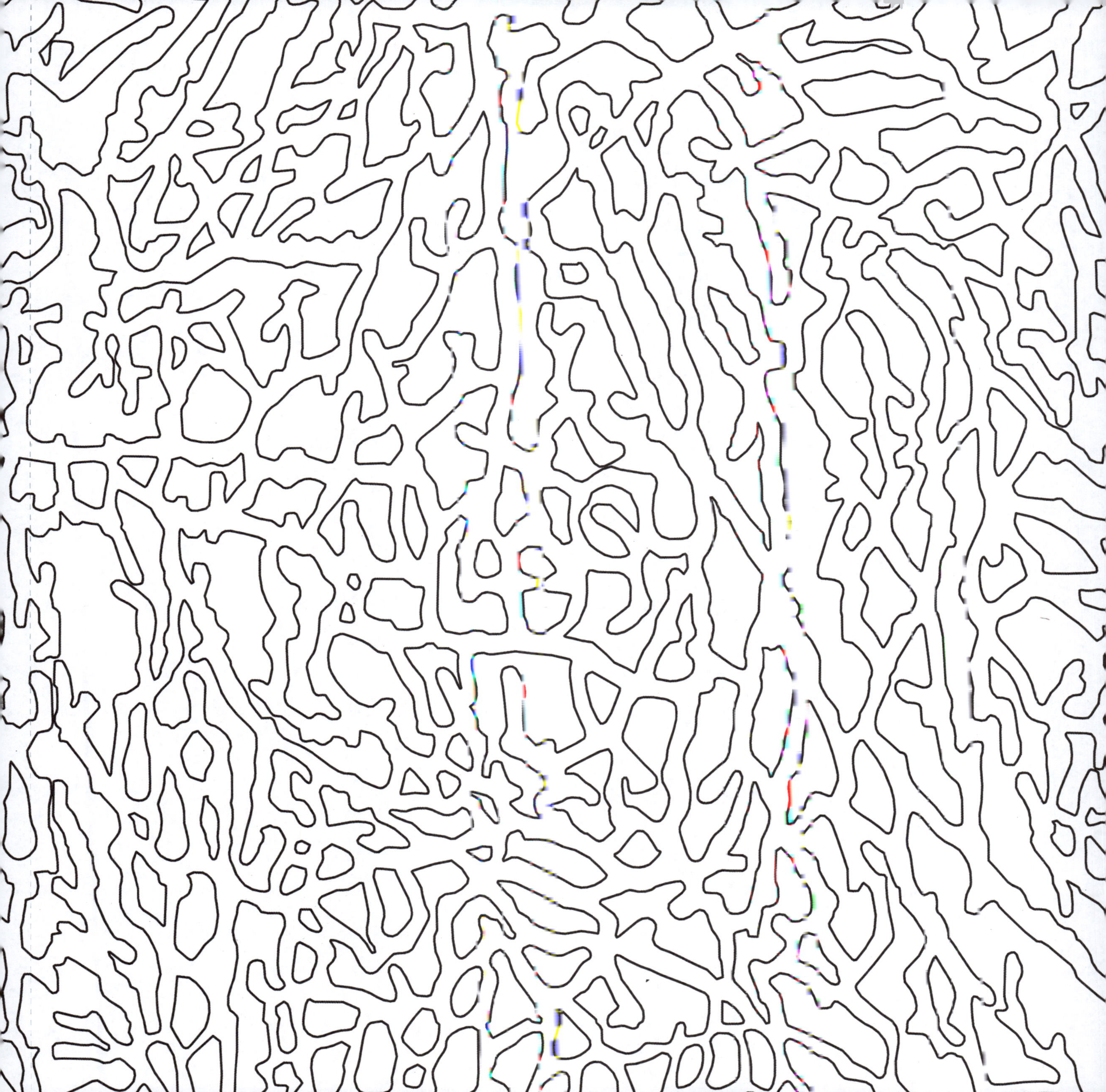

Top trunk Elephant Facts

1. Elephants are the world's largest land animal! African elephants can be 3 metres tall and Asian elephants can reach 2.7 metres in height!

2. Elephant tusks never stop growing. You can usually tell the age of an elephant by the length of their tusks.

3. Elephants spend between 12 to 18 hours a day eating grass, plants and fruit.

4. Elephants protect their skin from burning in the sun by throwing mud and sand over themselves.

Colour by Numbers

1 - light green	3 - blue	5 - pink	7 - yellow	9 - brown
2 - dark green	4 - grey	6 - purple	8 - orange	10 - white

Gorilla

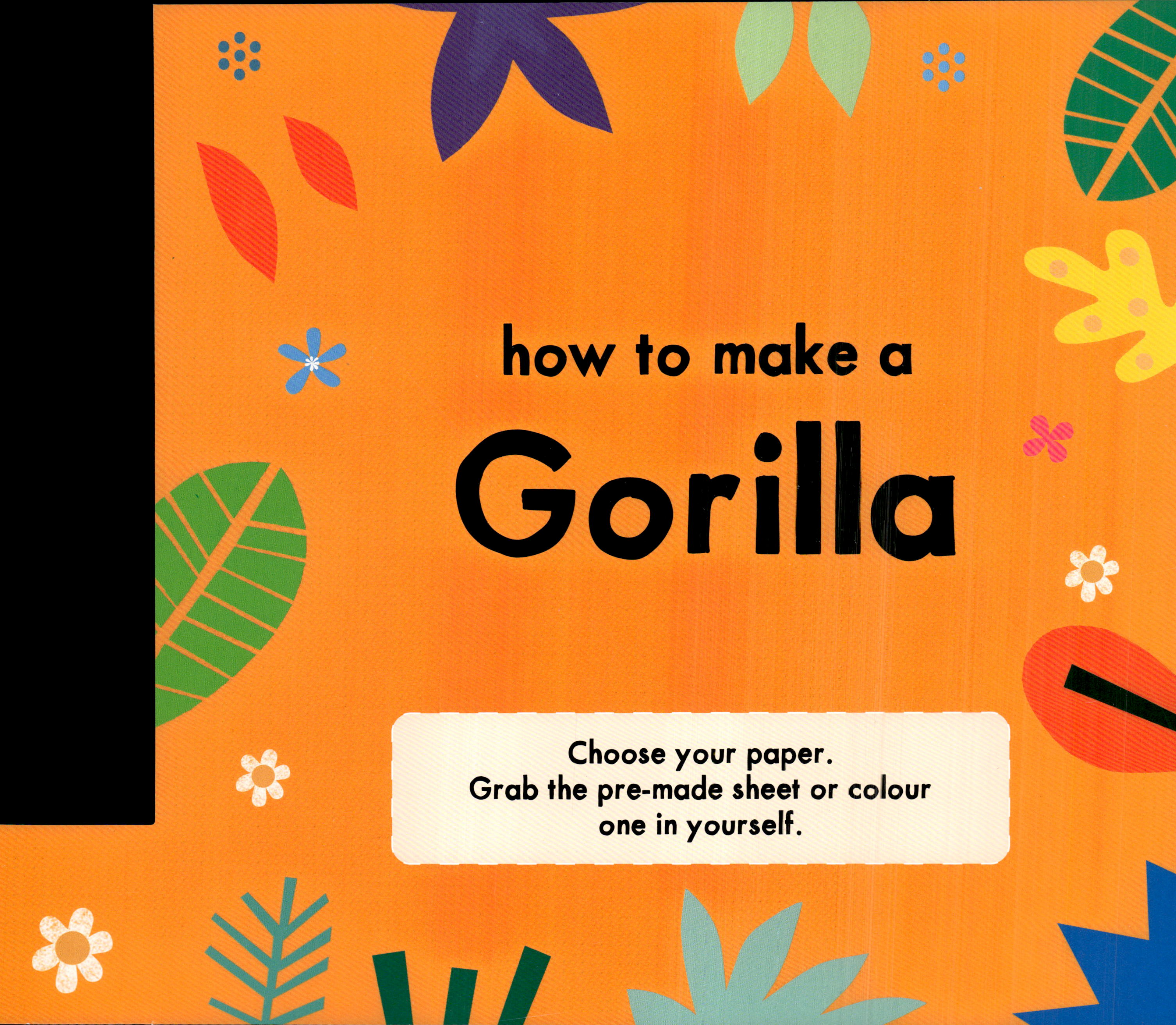
how to make a
Gorilla
Choose your paper.
Grab the pre-made sheet or colour
one in yourself.

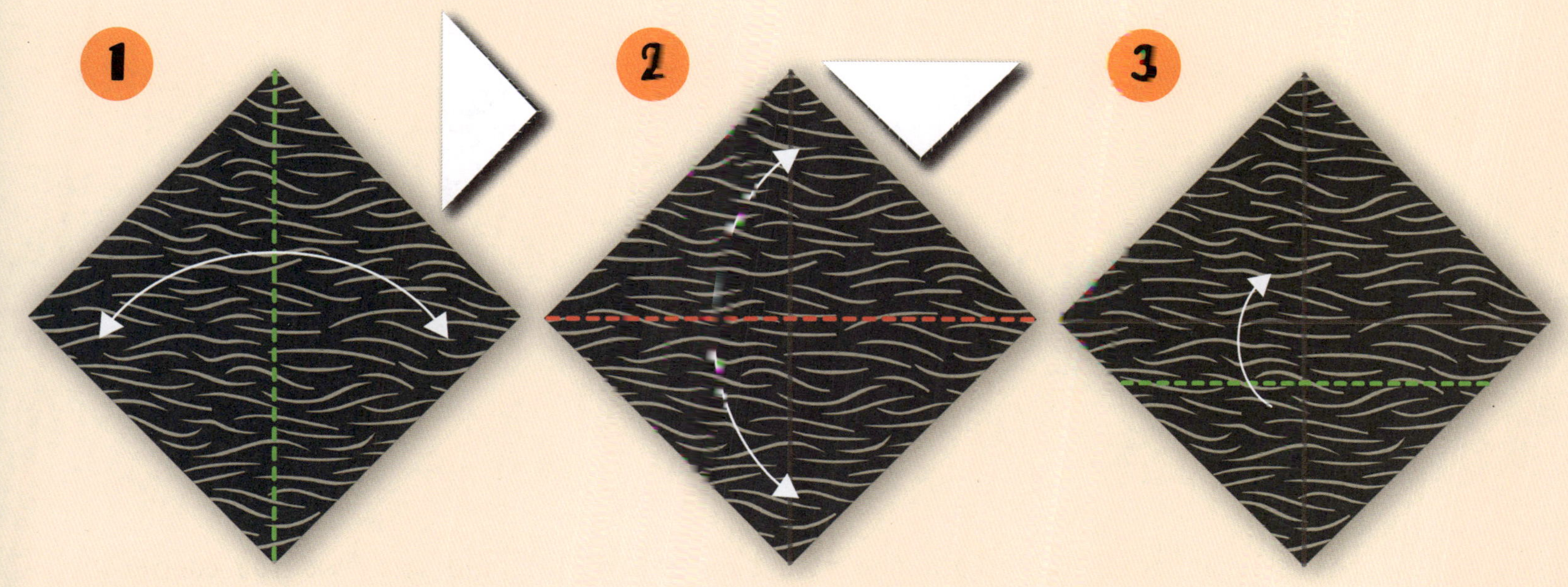

1. Fold the paper in half along the green dotted line, then open back up.

2. Fold the paper in half along the red dotted line, then open back up.

3. Fold the bottom half of the paper up along the green dotted line.

4

6

4. Fold the top corner of the paper down backwards along the red dotted line.

5. Fold the top corner of the paper down backwards along the green dotted line.

6. Turn the paper over.

7

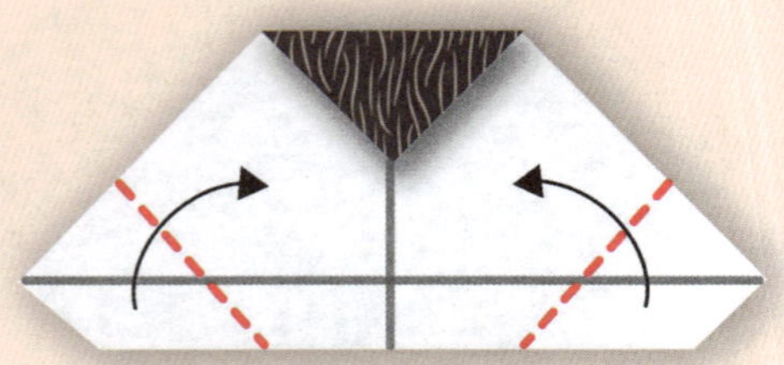

Fold the two bottom corners of the paper in along the red dotted lines.

8

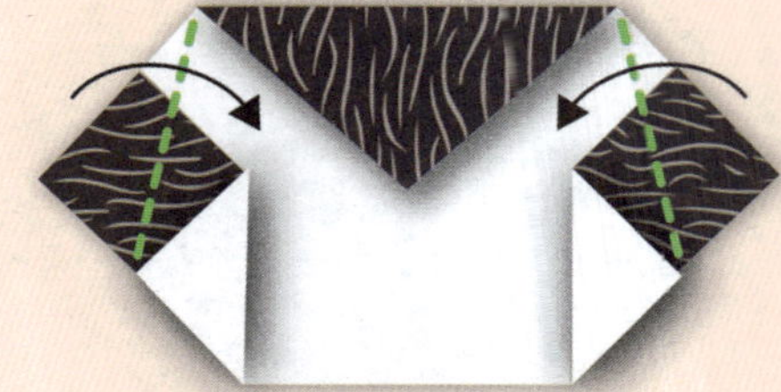

Fold the two sides of the paper in along the green dotted lines.

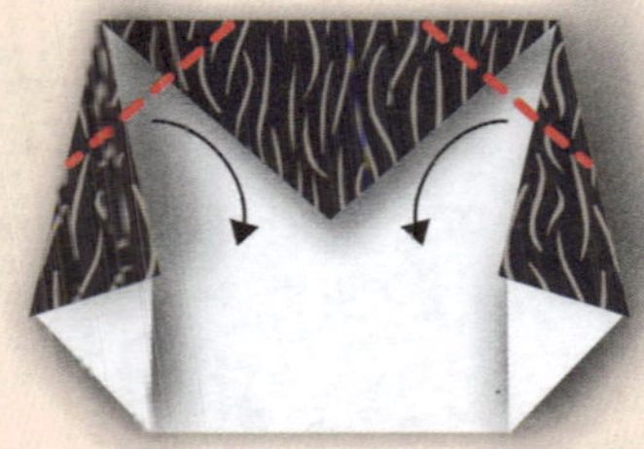

Fold the two top corners of the paper in along the red dotted lines.

Fold up the two top corners of the paper along the green dotted lines.

11

Turn the paper back over.

12

Well done! You've made the shape of the gorilla's face!

Add stickers to finish it off.

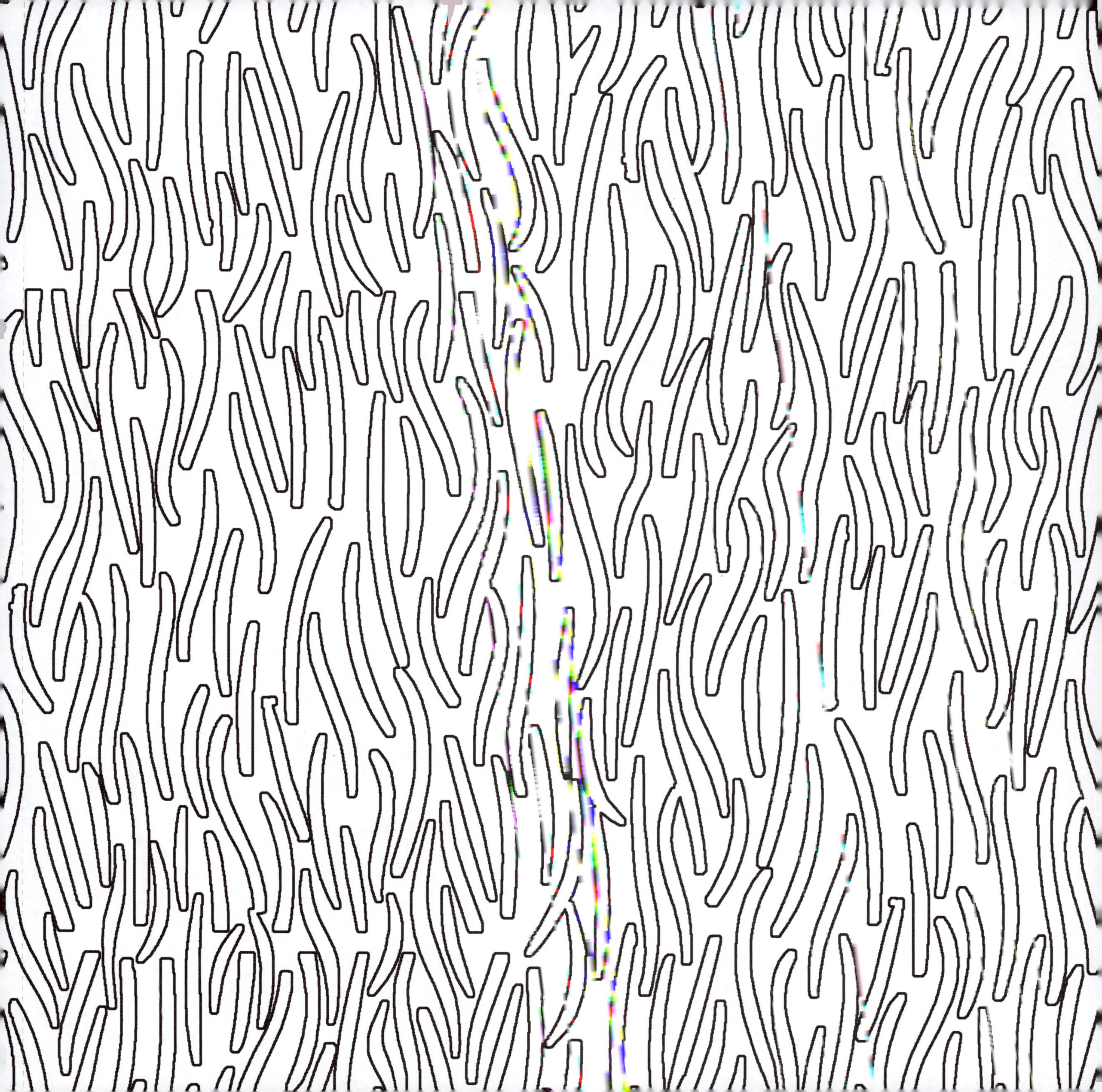

Fun Facts about gorillas

1. Gorillas can weigh over 200 kilos and they can grow as tall as an average human!

2. Gorillas are very clever animals. They have been seen using and making tools!

3. A female gorilla named Koko learned over 1,000 signs in sign language and was able to understand more than 2,000 English words!

4. All gorillas have unique nose prints!

Gorilla Maze

Can you help the gorilla find his way to the bananas?

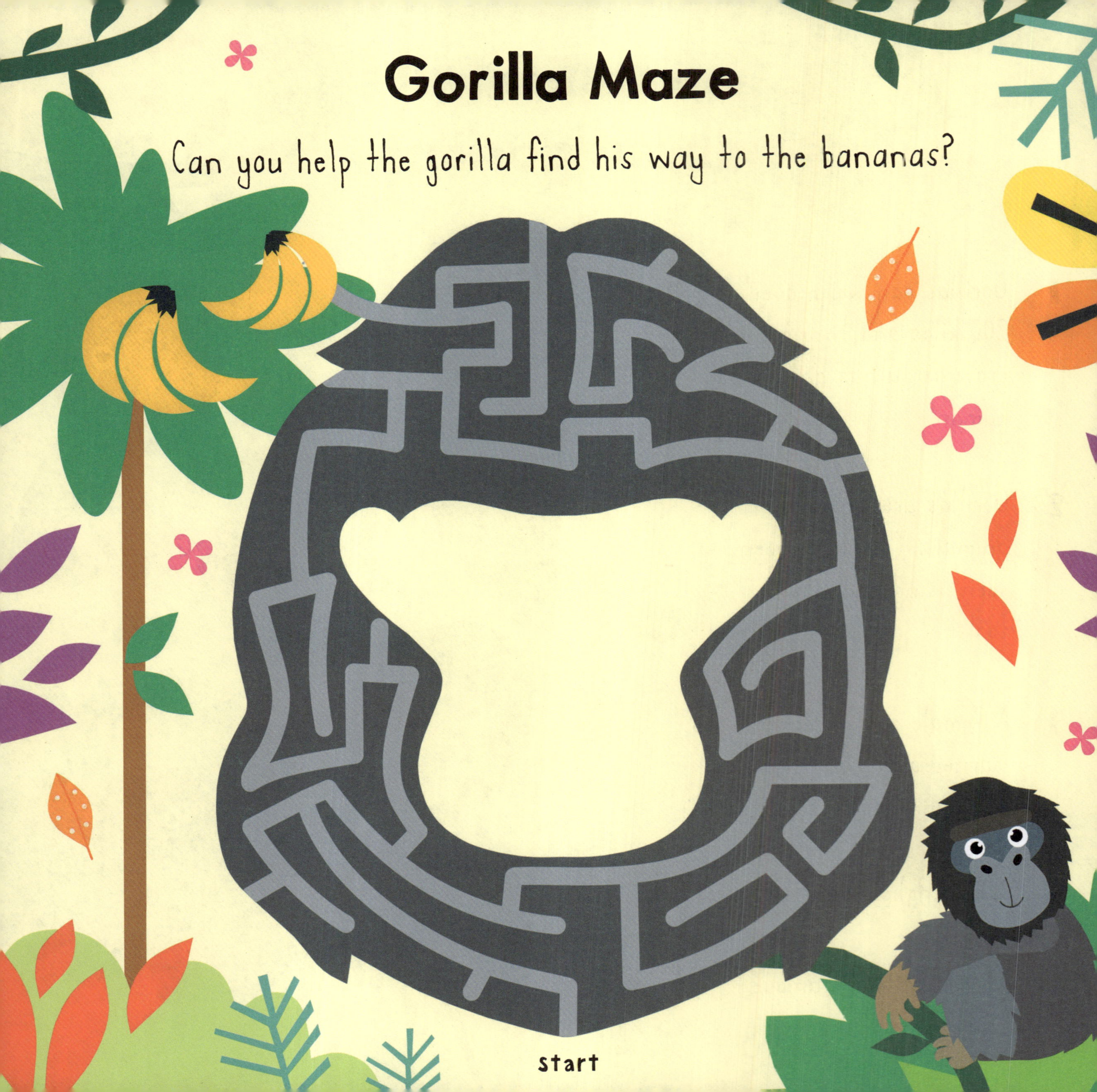

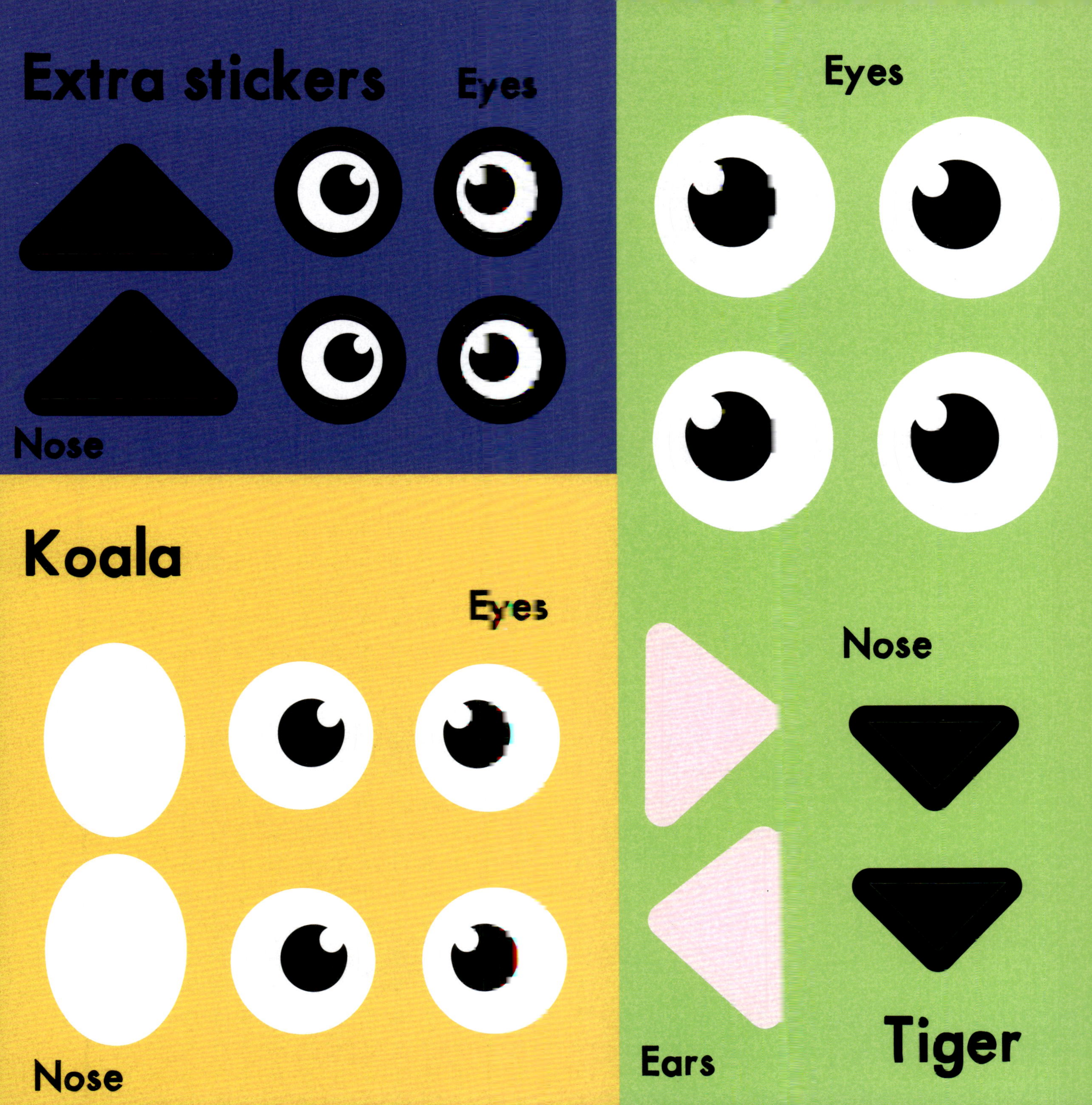
Extra stickers
Eyes
Nose
Eyes
Koala
Eyes
Nose
Nose
Ears
Tiger

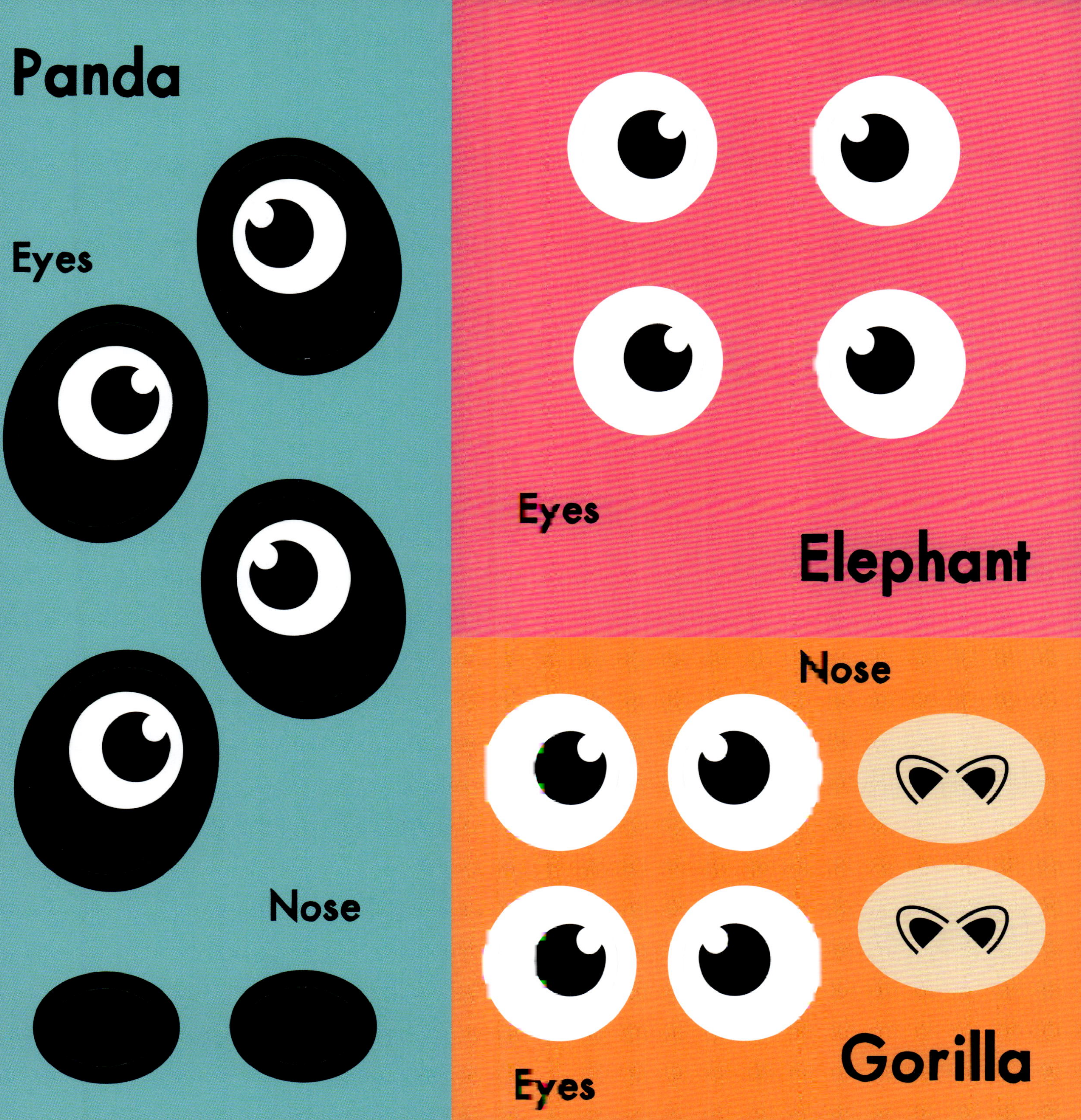
Panda
Eyes
Nose
Eyes
Elephant
Nose
Eyes
Gorilla